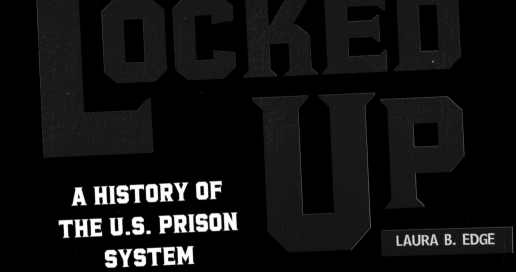

LOCKED UP

A HISTORY OF THE U.S. PRISON SYSTEM

LAURA B. EDGE

TWENTY-FIRST CENTURY BOOKS
MINNEAPOLIS

Dedicated to Chris, Doris, Judith, Lynne, Miriam, Monica, and Tammy, my incredibly talented critique group, for their encouragement and support.

Many thanks to Diane and Brent Oxner, Jim Kennedy of *Economic Opportunities*, Israel Cason of *I Can't We Can*, and the dedicated staff of the Kingwood Library for their invaluable help with research.

Quotation page 15, reprinted by permission of the publisher from *New Travels in the United States of America, 1788*, by J. P. Brissot de Warville, edited by Durand Echeverria, translated by Mara Soceanu Vamos and Durand Echeverria, p. 296, Cambridge, Mass.: The Belknap Press of Harvard University Press, Copyright © 1964 by the President and Fellows of Harvard College. Copyright © renewed 1992 by Durand Echeverria, Editor.

Quotation page 53, from "Medicine in Prison," from *Warden Ragen of Joliet* by Gladys A. Erickson, copyright 1957 by E. P. Dutton & Co., Inc., © renewed 1985 by Gladys A. Erickson. Used by permission of Dutton, a division of Penguin Group (USA) Inc.

Twenty-First Century Books
A division of Lerner Publishing Group, Inc.
241 First Avenue North
Minneapolis, MN 55401 U.S.A.

Website address: www.lernerbooks.com

Library of Congress Cataloging-in-Publication Data

Edge, Laura Bufano, 1953-
    Locked up : a history of the U.S. prison system / by Laura B. Edge.
        p.   cm. — (People's history)
    Includes bibliographical references and index.
    ISBN 978–0–8225–8750–7 (lib. bdg. : alk. paper)
    1. Prisons—United States—History. 2. Punishment—United States—History. 3. Prisoners—United States—Social conditions—History. I. Title.
    HV9466.E34 2009
    365'.973—dc22   2008026883

Manufactured in the United States of America
1 2 3 4 5 6 – BP – 14 13 12 11 10 09

CHAPTER ONE

EVERY CRIME A SIN, EVERY SIN A CRIME

In September 1773, twenty-one-year-old Levi Ames of Boston, Massachusetts, confessed to being a member of a gang of robbers. He stood trial and was found guilty of burglary. Ames was sentenced to be hanged on October 21. Newspapers reported that between seven and eight thousand people turned out to listen to his last words and to watch his execution.

In legal terms, crime is an action that a society views as wrong. It is an action that is punishable by law. Serious crimes, such as murder, are called felonies. Minor crimes, such as traffic violations, are called misdemeanors. The U.S. government and every state in the United States have lists of punishments for various types of crimes. But attitudes about what is considered a crime have changed over time. For the Puritans, a strict Christian sect in New England, lying and idleness were crimes. In the 1920s, making and selling alcoholic beverages was against the law. Judgments about how to punish criminals have also changed through the years.

SEND THEM TO THE COLONIES

In the 1600s and 1700s, many crimes in England were punishable by death. The most common method of execution was by hanging. Over time, the crime rate rose and the number of hangings increased. British officials decided it was wasteful to execute so many people. The American colonists were struggling to plant crops and build towns. If British criminals worked in the colonies, Britain would get rid of its "undesirables" and the American colonies would gain much-needed workers. In 1718 Parliament (the British lawmaking body) passed the Transportation Act. The act allowed British judges to transport convicts to the American colonies instead of sentencing them to death.

According to historian A. Roger Ekirch, "Well over 30,000 convicts boarded ships in England for transportation to America from the beginning of the trade in 1718 to its end in 1775." Prisoners were sent to the colonies to work, usually for seven or fourteen years. The number of years depended on the crime committed. Afterward, they could either stay in the colonies or return to Britain. They performed various types of jobs. Tobacco was an important crop in colonial America, and British prisoners often worked on tobacco plantations. A convict named John Winter painted George Washington's home at Mount Vernon, his Virginia plantation.

Many colonists were against convict transportation. In the *Pennsylvania Gazette*, Benjamin Franklin called the policy "an insult and contempt, the cruellest perhaps that ever one people offered another." Franklin thought the colonists ought to repay the British prime minister and members of Parliament for the policy. He suggested the colonists send rattlesnakes to Britain and scatter them in their gardens. The American Revolution (1775–1783) put an end to prisoner transportation.

COLONIAL CRIME AND PUNISHMENT

Colonial attitudes about living were strongly influenced by the Christian Bible. Colonists linked crime with sin. Punishment for crime was based on the Old Testament principle of vengeance. Colonists believed that punishment was a way to bring the sinner back to a right relationship with God. When the sinner's relationship with God was restored, that person would stop committing crimes.

The colonial system of criminal justice was based on the laws of Great Britain. The British legal system is known as English common law. Most punishments in colonial America resembled those of English common law, but they were less severe. For example, in Britain a person convicted of a property crime, such as theft or burglary, faced a swift march to the gallows. In colonial America, on the other hand, capital punishment (the death penalty) was used less often for these crimes.

Colonial punishments were public. Lying, swearing, name-calling, or skipping Sunday church worship could be punished by whipping. The whipping post, often painted red, stood in the most public street in town. In addition to the physical pain of the punishment, criminals had to face the stares of their neighbors. In these small communities, everyone knew his or her neighbor and the neighbor's business. Shame and embarrassment were powerful tools for controlling crime. The aim was to teach the sinners a lesson and make them want to repent.

Two other common colonial punishments were the stocks and the pillory. The stocks were made of heavy wooden planks with holes cut out for the prisoner's hands and feet. Offenders sat in the stocks, unable to move or defend themselves. Bystanders pelted the person with rotten eggs, fruit, vegetables, mud, or even stones. In 1656 Captain Kemble of Boston sat in the stocks for two hours because of "lewd and unseemly behavior" on the Sabbath. His crime was kissing his wife on Sunday. He had just returned from three years at sea.

The pillory was an upright, hinged board with holes for the head and hands. The offender's ears were often nailed to the pillory, and the prisoner was usually whipped. Those forced to stand in the pillory often had to wear a sign to advertise their crime. According to a Virginia statute (law) of 1748, the punishment for stealing a hog was "twenty-five lashes and a fine; the second offense meant two hours in the pillory, nailed by the ears, plus a fine. The third offense brought death."

A common punishment for women was the ducking stool. It was used to punish gossips and women who scolded their husbands. The woman was strapped to a chair and dipped into a river or stream. Onlookers jeered from the bank, adding to the woman's humiliation.

Colonists often had to wear shame letters to warn the community of their criminal behavior. For the crime of drunkenness, for

This early nineteenth-century American wood engraving shows a man being punished in the pillory.

example, a person could be whipped or ordered to wear a large *D* on his or her clothes. Nathaniel Hawthorne's classic novel, *The Scarlet Letter* (1850), describes this colonial practice. The book's main character, Hester Prynne, is forced to wear a scarlet *A* as punishment for adultery. Sometimes shame letters were branded onto the hand or forehead of the offender. For example, a branded *T* permanently identified a person as a thief. Repeat offenders were banished from the community. If they returned, they faced death.

In Puritan Massachusetts, colonists were expected to attend daily church services. A woman who skipped a church service might be forced

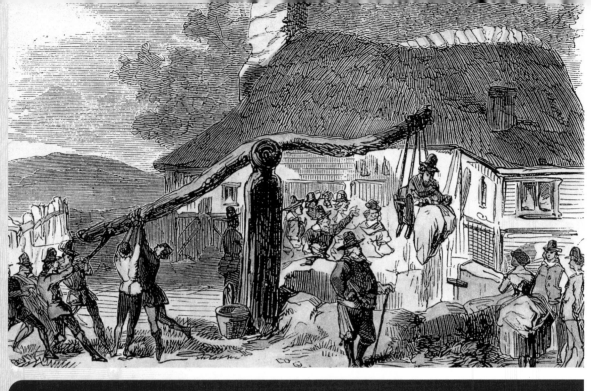

Colonists who came to America from England brought with them the practice of using ducking stools as punishment for women.

to stand in front of the church with a large sign around her neck to announce her sin. Other penalties for missing church were fines and prison. Offenders who repeatedly missed Sunday service faced the death penalty, usually by hanging.

DIFFERENT STROKES FOR DIFFERENT FOLKS

Many colonial laws carried different punishments depending on who committed the crime. Ministers were rarely whipped or put in the stocks. Neither were wealthy, upper-class offenders. Instead, they were fined. Corporal (physical) punishments were for the poorest members of the community. Servants, slaves, and laborers were punished in this way.

Slaves were whipped at their master's discretion. On December 18, 1712, William Byrd II of Westover, Virginia, noted in his diary, "I found Eugene [Byrd's slave] asleep instead of being at work, for which I beat him severely."

Byrd's wife, Lucy, was even harsher than her husband when it came to punishing slaves. His diary recorded several examples of her cruelty. She whipped her slave Prue violently and beat Jenny with fire tongs.

WILLIAM PENN AND THE QUAKER CODE

A religious group called the Quakers faced violent persecution in England, their homeland. They came to New England, where they hoped to practice their faith freely. But the Puritans persecuted them as well. So William Penn, an English Quaker, founded a new American colony, Pennsylvania. Here colonists could enjoy religious freedom. Penn did not allow atheists and nonbelievers in his new colony. Everyone else could practice his or her faith in peace.

The Quakers did not agree with the harsh physical punishments of colonial America. They did not believe it was right to take a human life. William Penn estab-

This early nineteenth-century drawing shows a white woman whipping a slave at a whipping post.

lished a penal code (a system of laws that define crimes and their punishments) for Pennsylvania. In Penn's code, only premeditated murder and treason could be punished by the death penalty. All other crimes would be punished by hard labor. Penn's Great Law stated that offenders should be imprisoned in houses of correction. "They would be required to perform useful work in compensation for, and in proportion to, their crimes." When Penn died in 1718, Pennsylvania's new leaders brought the criminal code of English common law to the state. Corporal punishment and the greater use of the death penalty were put in place in Pennsylvania.

COLONIAL JAILS

The earliest colonial jails were holding cells for debtors (people who owe money and can't pay their bills). Jails also held vagrants (wandering homeless people) and criminals awaiting trial. Jail time was brief. Each person's labor was important to the community. A town would not survive if too many people sat in jail and did not do their share of the work. After trial, the prisoner was either set free, fined, punished, or executed.

As towns grew, crime increased. Communities became more impersonal, and people no longer knew the details of their neighbor's lives. Poverty and unemployment caused some people to turn to crime as a way to survive. Pickpockets were common on market days. Petty thievery, housebreaking, burglary, highway robbery, assault, and murder became more common.

Jails filled with debtors, light offenders, and hardened criminals. Men, women, and children were thrown into cells together. Prisoners were sometimes chained to the floor or wall. Overcrowding and horrendous conditions resulted. According to a report by the Boston Prison Discipline Society:

> The old and the young, the novice [inexperienced] in guilt and the veteran in crime, the mere vagrant and the highway robber, the heedless [thoughtless] trespasser and the deliberate murderer, were herded together in close and dirty rooms, and were left without employment, without instruction, without even the decencies of life.

Colonial jails were smelly, crowded, and dark. Prisoners suffered from freezing cold in the winter and blistering heat in the summer. Rats, fleas, and other vermin caused the spread of contagious diseases. Many prisoners became sick and died. Beds and bedding were usually not provided to prisoners. They had to rely on charity for their basic needs. Jailers charged prisoners for their room and board. Those without money often starved. Daniel Fowle was sent to Boston's stone prison in 1754 for printing a pamphlet that angered authorities. He wrote, "If there is any such thing as a hell upon earth, I think this place is the nearest resemblance of any I can conceive of."

DEBTORS

Debtors were often sent to jail until they could pay their bills. If a debtor owned property, he was allowed to turn it over to his creditors (the people to whom he owed money). Then the debtor would be released from prison. In some colonies, debtors could leave their cell during the day to work or beg on the streets. They returned to prison at night.

Many community leaders were concerned about the treatment of debtors. In moral terms, debtors were not criminals. They had not committed a criminal act. They were just poor people who could not pay their bills. Most of them had families. Men imprisoned for debt had to leave their wives and children while they served their prison terms. This placed great stress on colonial families, since women and children had few opportunities to earn money. In 1776 the Philadelphia Society for Assisting Distressed Prisoners was formed to improve the lives of prisoners, especially debtors. Society members pushed a canvas-covered wheelbarrow through the streets of Philadelphia. They went from house to house and gathered food and clothing for prisoners.

ON CRIMES AND PUNISHMENTS

About this time, Cesare Beccaria, an Italian aristocrat and economist, wrote a small, influential book called *On Crimes and Punishments*. Beccaria believed it was better to prevent crimes than to punish them. "A punishment, to be just, should have only that degree of severity which is sufficient to deter [discourage] others," he wrote.

Beccaria believed in the humane treatment of criminals. He wanted to end torture and the death penalty. He also wanted to give all accused people the right to defend themselves in court. Beccaria considered swift and equal punishments for all to be more effective than severe penalties. He believed in imprisonment as an effective punishment for crime.

Another progressive thinker of the time, John Howard of Great Britain, pioneered prison reform. In the mid 1770s, he toured prisons in Britain. His book, *The State of the Prisons in England and Wales*, described his findings. He thought prisons should provide decent food and clean, separate cells for prisoners. Howard thought prisons should encourage inmates to regret their crimes. He introduced into English the word *penitentiary*, meaning "prison." This new word stemmed from the idea that prisons should be places where lawbreakers become penitent, or sorry, for their mistakes.

As the 1700s came to a close, Americans began to realize that harsh physical punishments failed to stop crime. The writings of Beccaria, Howard, and other reformers changed the direction of the American penal system. Their progressive ideas led to a shift from corporal punishment to imprisonment as the main form of punishing crimes. The result was the modern penitentiary.

Prisons are destructive of
the health, liberty, and
goodness of man.

—J. P. BRISSOT DE WARVILLE, FRENCH WRITER AND DIPLOMAT,
AFTER VISITING U.S. PRISONS, 1788

CHAPTER TWO

SILENT AND SEPARATE

After the American Revolution, U.S. leaders looked carefully at colonial laws and thought about ways to improve them. They reduced the number of crimes against morality. For example, missing church on Sunday was no longer considered a crime. The death penalty was not used as often. U.S. leaders based the criminal justice system on the ideals of liberty and the good of the people. If a person's actions interfered with another person's well-being, then that person would be punished in some way.

During this time, people became more mobile. Cities grew dramatically, and communities filled with newcomers. The national economy was in a depression, or a serious decline. Jobs were hard to find. This led to an increase in crime. As poverty and crime increased, attitudes changed about the sources of crime. The colonial view, which had seen crime as a result of individual weakness and sin influenced by the devil, gave way to the idea that a person's environment could lead to crime. People blamed crime on bad company, poor upbringing, lack of education, alcohol, and cities filled with vice.

Attitudes about punishment changed as well. Corporal punishment became much less effective. In cities of strangers, shame no longer played a role in controlling crime. Communities began to feel that the best form of punishment would be to remove the criminal from negative influences. If a person's surroundings caused a lapse into crime, then place that criminal in a corruption-free environment. As a result, punishment for crime gradually shifted from corporal punishment to imprisonment.

DR. BENJAMIN RUSH: CHAMPION FOR CHANGE

In 1787 Dr. Benjamin Rush and a small group of men met at Benjamin Franklin's home in Philadelphia. They discussed the problem of public punishments. Rush believed that "All *public* punishments tend to make bad men worse, and to increase crimes." He thought "crimes should be punished in private, or not punished at all." Rush felt that criminals could be reformed by incarceration (prison time), labor, and penitence. He worked hard to gather support for his ideas.

Rush's group developed a plan of reform for Pennsylvania. First, they changed the criminal code. They reduced the number of capital crimes (crimes punishable by death). They also sentenced criminals to imprisonment rather than to corporal punishment. Second, the group reduced the physical suffering of prisoners. They improved sanitary conditions in jails and prisons. And, finally, they developed a "separate system" of confinement and discipline for serious offenders. Under this system, prisoners would be separated from one another in prison. In 1790 the Pennsylvania legislature (lawmaking body) passed a bill that called for the Walnut Street Jail in Philadelphia to be remodeled to include a penitentiary house.

THE WALNUT STREET JAIL

The remodeled Walnut Street Jail opened in 1790. It was the first penitentiary in the United States. The brick prison was three stories high and was surrounded by a 20-foot-high (6-meter) wall. Walnut was designed to reform convicted felons. Its goal was to rehabilitate prisoners, or restore them to crime-free lives.

Walnut housed prisoners from all parts of Pennsylvania. Serious offenders were separated from those who had committed less serious crimes. Minor criminals slept in large dormitories. During the day, they worked together in shops. Male prisoners made shoes, tailored clothes, and made nails. Female prisoners spun cotton, did laundry, and mended clothes.

U.S. artist William Russell Birch created this painting of the Walnut Street Jail *(white building on right)* in Philadelphia in 1799.

Serious offenders were kept in solitary confinement. They were allowed to read the Bible and to think about their crimes and repent. These prisoners were given no labor to break up the monotony of their days. Those who supported the idea of solitary confinement believed it prevented the spread of bad habits that occurred when inmates were allowed to mix freely. They also believed that isolation and silence would force prisoners to think about their crimes. This reflection would reform convicts and turn them into productive citizens. Prison officials soon learned that inmates suffered physically and mentally from solitary confinement. Work was introduced as a privilege that inmates could earn through good behavior.

Hard work and humane treatment were the guiding principles at Walnut. Officials sought to meet the prisoners' educational needs as well as their physical needs. They opened a school in 1798. Inmates received basic instruction in reading, writing, and arithmetic. Walnut also focused on Christian religious training for inmates. All prisoners were required to meet for Sunday worship. The Philadelphia Prison Society provided books, such as *Power of Religion on the Mind, A Serious Call to a Devout Life*, and *Jennings View of Christianity*, to improve inmates' moral character

By 1818 Walnut Street Jail was overcrowded. Yet many people thought the prison was a model of reform. The Pennsylvania legislature agreed to build two new penitentiaries, one in Pittsburgh and the other in Philadelphia. Lawmakers from other states passed similar legislation. Before long, penitentiaries were built in New York, Virginia, Massachusetts, Vermont, Maryland, and New Hampshire.

THOMAS EDDY: FATHER OF NEW YORK STATE PRISON

Thomas Eddy, a New York businessman and philanthropist, visited the Walnut Street Jail in the 1790s. He returned to New York to help draft the New York penal code and to design a prison system for the state. The result was Newgate Prison, built on the east bank of the Hudson River in New York City. Inmates were provided food and clothing at no cost.

Corporal punishment was not allowed. Each of the prison's fifty-four rooms held eight people, and prisoners slept two to a bed.

Eddy served as principal keeper, or warden, of Newgate for several years. He developed a system of labor that allowed prisoners to work together in small groups. He kept records of each inmate's production and conduct and offered rewards to encourage good behavior. After a short time, however, Eddy realized that housing several prisoners in one room was a mistake. Bloody riots and mass escapes convinced him of the need for separate cells for prisoners. According to Eddy, inmates needed to be isolated from one another. In that way, they could not spread loose morals or come up with new plans of corruption. Kept apart, they would repent and reform. With these ideas in mind, Eddy began to plan a new prison at Auburn, in northern New York State. At Auburn, prisoners would not be able to corrupt one another.

Thomas Eddy was the first significant prison reformer in New York. This engraving by Samuel I. Knapp is from the mid-nineteenth century.

AUBURN: THE SILENT SYSTEM

Auburn Prison opened in 1821. The Auburn system was based on silence, separation, and hard labor. It also included rigid discipline and corporal punishment for those who broke the rules. At Auburn, prisoners worked in silence with other prisoners during the day. They were confined to separate cells at night. Those who broke the rules or caused trouble were placed full-time in solitary cells or dungeons. According to the board of inspectors of Auburn Prison:

> Let them have pure air, wholesome food, comfortable clothing, and medical aid when necessary; cut them off from all intercourse [communication] with men; let not the voice

or face of a friend ever cheer them; let them walk their gloomy abodes [cells], and commune with their corrupt hearts and guilty consciences in silence, and brood over the horrors of their solitude, and the enormity of their crimes, without the hope of . . . pardon.

Auburn enforced strict discipline. Talking and all other forms of communication were not allowed between prisoners. Convicts cast their eyes downward and marched in lockstep to meals. They ate at narrow tables with their backs toward the center of the room. Seated this way they could not make eye contact or exchange signs with other prisoners. In addition to the silence inside the prison walls, prisoners were not allowed any communication with the outside world.

To maintain strict discipline, prisoners were flogged, or beaten with rawhide whips, if they talked or broke prison rules. According to Elam Lynds, director of Auburn in the 1820s, "I consider the chastisement [punishment] by the whip, the most efficient, and, at the same time, the most humane which exists. . . . I consider it impossible to govern a large prison without a whip."

Pennsylvania legislators (lawmakers) took Auburn's idea of silence and separation one step further. They developed a similar but distinct mode of prison discipline, the separate system, at Eastern State Penitentiary in Philadelphia.

EASTERN STATE PENITENTIARY: THE SEPARATE SYSTEM

Eastern State Penitentiary began housing prisoners in 1829. The prison was an engineering marvel. It was the largest and most expensive public building in the United States at that time. Thirty-foot (9 m) stone walls surrounded seven cell blocks that branched out from a central hub like the spokes of a wheel. Architect John Haviland designed Eastern to look like a medieval castle. It was forbidding, somber, and bleak. The building commission approved, stating, "The exterior of a solitary prison should exhibit as much as possible great strength and convey to the mind a cheerless blank indicative of the misery that awaits the unhappy being who enters within its walls."

Eastern became the model for the separate, or solitary, system of prison discipline. The prison was designed to prevent communication between prisoners. Inmates were housed in separate cells with small private exercise yards. Each cell was furnished with water, plumbing, and heat and was large enough for the prisoner and his work equipment. Prisoners were not allowed to leave their cells at all during their sentences. They worked, ate, and slept alone. Prison officials were convinced that, if left alone with their thoughts, prisoners would seek the light of God through prayer and meditation. "Each individual," explained an Eastern supporter, "will necessarily

Eastern State Penitentiary in Pennsylvania was designed and run as a solitary prison. Inmates had no

be made the instrument of his own punishment; his conscience will be the avenger of society."

When a new prisoner arrived at Eastern, he was assigned a number, his hair was cut short, and he was given a coarse cotton uniform. A black hood was placed over his head so that he would not see or be seen by other inmates as he was led to his cell. British novelist Charles Dickens visited the prison in 1842. He wrote about his observations in the book *American Notes* (1842):

> Over the head and face of every prisoner who comes into this melancholy house, a black hood is drawn; and in this dark shroud, an emblem of the curtain dropped between him and the living world, he is led to the cell from which he never again comes forth, until his whole term of imprisonment has expired. He never hears of wife and children; home or friends; the life or death of any single creature. He sees the prison-officers, but with that exception he never looks upon a human countenance [face], or hears a human voice. He is a man buried alive; to be dug out in the slow round of years; and in the meantime dead to everything but torturing anxieties and horrible despair.

Like other prison officials at this time, Eastern guards severely punished inmates who broke the rules. Offenders were often thrown into dark, rat-infested punishment cells that looked like medieval dungeons. Some were given a water bath, which involved pouring buckets of cold water over a naked prisoner from a great height until icicles formed on his head or body.

WHICH IS BEST: SILENT OR SEPARATE?

Some people thought the Auburn system of prison management was the best way to run a prison. Others supported the Eastern system. Social reformers from around the world visited both prisons. They wrote articles and pamphlets supporting one system or the other. Both groups felt they had found the winning formula that would cause convicts to reflect on their past mistakes and transform into law-abiding citizens.

Both systems revolved around the separation of prisoners, silence, strict obedience to rules, and labor. Yet Eastern's separate-cell prison design was far more expensive to build and operate than was Auburn's design. Profits from prison labor were also higher at Auburn. Prisoners who worked together produced more goods than prisoners who worked alone. As a result, by the 1840s, Auburn's silent system became the pattern for the majority of prisons built in the United States in the 1800s.

FALLEN WOMEN

Throughout history, women have faced economic hardships. In the industrial age, their job options were limited and they found it difficult to earn a living. To support themselves, some women in the 1800s turned to theft or prostitution. Society shunned them and called them fallen women. These women were arrested and imprisoned for crimes against decency.

In the 1800s, society considered women to be morally superior to men. They were thought to be naturally honest and good. When women broke the law, they were thought to have acted against their natural purity. As a result, women convicts were considered worse than male convicts. Many people thought these women could not be reformed. British prison reformer Mary Carpenter wrote in 1864, "Female Convicts are, as a class, even more morally degraded than men." In the early penitentiaries, women prisoners were locked in large rooms. They stayed in those rooms for their entire sentences. Guards delivered food and needlework to their cells. Women prisoners were often attacked and abused by their male guards.

The issue of prisoners, both male and female, soon faded into the background. The Civil War (1861–1865) stopped thoughts of prison reform. The nation, ripped apart by war, struggled to hold itself together. It wasn't until the war ended that reformers once again turned their attention to the question of how to deal with people who broke the law.

> Rewards, more than punishments,
> are essential to every
> good prison system.
>
> —DECLARATION OF PRINCIPLES, NATIONAL PRISON CONGRESS, 1870

CHAPTER THREE

THE REFORM MOVEMENT

At the end of the Civil War in 1865, the American South lay in ruins. Crops were destroyed, cities were burned to the ground, and many roads and railroads no longer existed. Four million southern slaves were suddenly free. They had no property and no way of making a living. Their job experience was often limited to working on cotton plantations. Many fled rural areas and headed for cities in the North.

A surge of Irish, Italian, Jewish, and Chinese immigrants also flocked to the industrial cities of the North. Factories there, no longer needing to manufacture war goods, slowed production. They could not absorb all the new workers. As a result, slums and ghettos filled with poor and jobless people. They became breeding grounds for crime. As crime increased, so did anxiety and fear. Many white, native-born Americans saw crime as a problem created by freed African Americans and foreigners.

As the crime rate rose, prisons became overcrowded. The strict rules of prison life that had once helped to maintain order crumbled. Prisons became more brutal and corrupt. Prisoner unrest increased and with it came an increase in severe punishments for those who broke the rules. Released prisoners often committed additional crimes and wound up back in prison. Patrick Murphy, an Idaho prisoner in solitary confinement, wrote about his experience in prison:

> In the loneliness of that cell, with all the world seemingly against me, without even the sympathy of 'cons' [convicts] like myself, who were shut out from everything worthwhile in life, was born a feeling of resentment against the whole scheme of life. My heart was teeming with hate, my soul was seared with revenge and the perspiration of despair that trickled from my temples would have poisoned a rattlesnake.

But criminal justice experts firmly believed in prisons for reforming criminals. They just needed to find a better system of prison management.

WORKING ON A CHAIN GANG

The Fourteenth Amendment to the U.S. Constitution, passed in 1868, had guaranteed newly freed slaves equal protection under the law. But racial prejudice was still widespread. In the South, former slaves were arrested and thrown into prison more often than whites. Most southern prisons had been damaged or destroyed during the Civil War. Conditions were wretched, and prisoner treatment was harsh. Overcrowding and the inability to pay the housing costs for so many prisoners led to a convict leasing system.

In the lease system, private contractors hired inmates to work outside the prison. The prisoners worked on road construction projects, picked cotton and fruit, or worked in the mines. The contractor was responsible for the prisoners. This situation created conflicts between the contractor's need to make a profit and the need to treat the prisoners well. The humane treatment of prisoners often fell by the wayside.

In Selma, Alabama, African Americans were placed in chain gangs for "using abusive language towards a white man" or "selling farm produce within the town limits." Convicts were shackled together with heavy chains. They wore striped uniforms so they would be easy to identify if they tried to escape. Prisoners lived in hot, filthy prison camps, often in little more than cages. The death rate from disease and accidents was high.

Prisoners in Georgia work on a chain gang in the early twentieth century. Chain gangs in the United States trace their history to the 1800s.

NATIONAL PRISON CONGRESS

New ideas about prisons and prison discipline began to spread through the nation. Prison reformers Enoch Wines and Theodore Dwight visited several state penitentiaries. They studied each prison and, in the late 1860s, published a report on the dreadful conditions they found. Wines wanted the world's prison experts to join together to create an ideal prison system. He played a key role in organizing the National Prison Congress, which met in Cincinnati, Ohio, in 1870.

Delegates from twenty-four states, Canada, and South America attended the congress. Prison reformer Zebulon Reed Brockway gave a key speech. "The central aim of a true prison system is the protection of society against crime, not the punishment of the criminals," he told his listeners. Brockway shared his new ideas for reformation, or changing the character of the criminal. He defined reformation as a process that turns convicts into useful citizens.

The National Prison Congress adopted the Declaration of Principles. The principles were designed to reform convicts. They included religious instruction, education, and work. They also included a plan for supervising convicts after their release from prison. The congress believed that prisoners would reform if they knew that their actions and behavior determined when they got out of prison. Reformers supported a system where inmates worked their way through different stages of imprisonment. Each stage gave them more privileges and fewer restrictions. Eventually, prisoners would earn a conditional release from prison called parole.

Central to the reform policy was a new way of sentencing criminals known as the indeterminate sentence. In this new method, lawmakers set broad sentence ranges for each crime. During an offender's trial, a judge would then choose the minimum and maximum prison term within that range. So, instead of being sent to prison for a specific length of time, a criminal would go to prison for an indefinite period. Behavior while in prison would determine the length of time served.

Under the indeterminate system, parole boards and prison guards decided on the prisoner's actual release date. If a prisoner's behavior convinced the parole board that he or she would not commit future crimes, the prisoner was released early. If reform was not evident, the prisoner served a longer sentence. The goal was to give inmates a sense that their behavior controlled their fate. Although the congress had no formal authority to apply these ideas, the group's Declaration of Principles was a huge step toward prison reform.

WAYWARD WOMEN

Female inmates made up a small segment of the prison population in the United States of the 1800s. They were held in the same prisons as men. As a result, women were the victims of male prisoner violence on a regular basis. In the second half of the 1800s, small groups of middle- and upper-class women in New York, Massachusetts, and Indiana crusaded to build separate prisons for women. These reformers saw female convicts as "wayward girls" who had been led astray. They did not view them as fallen women, as had an earlier era. They believed that female offenders could be rehabilitated if they were kept away from the evil influence of men.

Reformers focused on three goals for women convicts. First, they wanted separate prisons for women. They also wanted to hire female staff to work in those prisons. And finally, they wanted to design special prison programs for females. According to a report of the superintendent of the Detroit House of Correction:

> Wayward women must be won to virtue by their own sex,
> if they are won at all. . . . Cultivate their natural love for
> home life; furnish them with womanly affection; fit them
> to earn an honest and sufficient support; find them employ-
> ment and a friend; follow them with friendly acts and faith-
> ful guardianship, and fear not for their future.

The Indiana Reformatory Institution for Women and Girls opened in

1873. It was the first prison completely devoted to and run by women. Prisoners learned domestic skills such as cooking, cleaning, laundering, sewing, and knitting. Before long, Massachusetts and New York also established women's prisons.

ELMIRA

In 1876 Zebulon Brockway got the chance to put his ideas for prison reform into practice. He became superintendent of the nation's first reformatory in Elmira, New York. Elmira housed male offenders from sixteen to thirty years old. They were all serving their first prison term. Brockway believed young, first-time offenders stood the greatest chance at true reform.

Elmira's goal was to reform convicts through rewards instead of punishments. Prisoners were classified and placed into one of three moral grades (first, second, and third). Inmates of the same grade were housed together and wore uniforms of the same color. Convicts earned better conditions and more privileges as they advanced through the grades. If they broke the rules or failed to work hard, they could be demoted to a lower grade. A new inmate entered Elmira in the second grade. After six months, his behavior and work were evaluated. Good behavior and hard work meant a promotion to the first grade and more privileges. If an inmate broke the rules or failed to work hard, he was given a coarse red uniform and demoted to the third grade. He had fewer privileges than prisoners in the other two grades.

The inmates received indeterminate sentences. They earned their way out of prison. When an inmate had learned and put into practice obedience, discipline, and a marketable trade skill, he was released. Prisoner Patrick Murphy thought the system motivated inmates to better themselves. "Good time for good conduct is a very powerful stimulant for discipline and obedience in prison," he wrote. "Hope is ever beckoning us on— even a 'lifer' [prisoner serving a life sentence] dreams of a day when things will be different."

Education was a large part of the Elmira system. According to Zebulon Brockway, "By education the whole man is toned up, and not only are the habits improved, but the quality of the mind itself." Educated inmates taught elementary classes. Chaplains and visiting teachers from Elmira College taught advanced classes. Bookkeeping, history, and literature were all part of Elmira's school.

At Elmira, inmates were kept busy all the time. They were meant to learn to be self-sufficient and to see the value of hard work. They also learned a trade. Some inmates worked at carpentry, plumbing, shoemaking, or brush making. Others worked at tailoring, drafting, sign painting, or weaving. The goods the prisoners made were sold for a profit outside the prison. According to New York district attorney Robert Drummond, "Integrity, thoroughness, honesty, accuracy, conscientiousness, faithfulness, patience—these unseen things which complete a soul are woven into the work."

Elmira prisoners received points for their work in the shops, at the school, and in moral conduct. As soon as an inmate earned enough points, he became a candidate for parole. Under the parole system, a prisoner was required to find a job at his trade when he was released from prison. He was given strict instructions for his behavior. These included avoiding criminal companions and alcoholic beverages. The parolee was closely monitored for six months. If, after that time, he proved his good behavior, he was discharged completely from the prison system.

Labor unions outside the prison criticized Elmira's work program. The unions wanted to restrict or eliminate convict labor. They thought prison labor brought unfair competition to law-abiding workers. As a result of pressure from the unions, New York lawmakers passed the Yates Law in 1888. The law banned machine, or industrial, labor in prisons. Prisoners were only allowed to produce goods by hand. For example, they could make brooms by hand. Hand labor did not compete directly with union labor. Prisoners were also only allowed to make items that could be sold to the State of New York. Brockway quickly began a physical education

program to take the place of hard labor at Elmira. Inmates learned military drills. They also played baseball, basketball, and football.

Elmira became the model for the reform movement in the last decades of the 1800s. Its programs were copied by many states. Eventually, though, some of Brockway's ideas became controversial. His work at Elmira had convinced him that low intelligence caused criminality. He felt that some convicts would never become law-abiding citizens. Serious overcrowding at Elmira limited many of his programs. It also made discipline difficult. An investigation into Elmira's punishment methods revealed an ugly truth. Whippings—although technically forbidden—were actually common for inmates who caused trouble or refused to work. They were especially common for inmates who had mental or physical disabilities.

Inmates at Elmira reformatory in New York learned military drills and discipline.

In addition to these problems, Elmira's educational program began to suffer. There were not enough teachers to meet the educational needs of the inmates. Also, convicts learned to pretend to reform. They acted and spoke in ways that convinced prison guards of their change in character. Once released from prison, they often returned to crime.

THE WILD WEST

As the United States expanded in the mid and late 1800s, western lands opened up to settlement. These new territories had limited law and order. Groups known as vigilantes tried to control crime by taking matters into their own hands. They hunted down criminals and hung them without the benefit of a trial. Other lawbreakers were thrown into makeshift jails to wait for their trials. For example, in a jail in the Oklahoma Territory, all prisoners were crammed together in a basement dungeon.

Convicts in the West were sent to prisons that were poorly constructed and grossly overcrowded. Inmates sat idle most of the time, and escapes were common. According to prisoner Pat Crowe, "After my release from the . . . penitentiary I took a diabolical [devilish] delight in holding up trains and dynamiting the express safe. I was a real, hard-boiled outlaw and glad of it, because I felt that anything I did was mild compared with the wrongs that society was inflicting on the men in its prisons."

JUVENILE OFFENDERS

Until the late 1800s, children who committed crimes could be arrested, tried, and sent to adult prisons in most states. Prison reformers realized that locking children and adults in the same prisons was a bad idea. It created schools of crime. Young offenders learned bad habits from hardened older criminals. They left prison knowing how to commit all kinds of unlawful acts.

In 1899 Julia Lathrop and a group of women in Chicago, Illinois, took action. They pressured Illinois legislators to create a separate court for children under the age of sixteen. The result, the Juvenile Court Act, established the first juvenile court in the United States. Child savers believed that early intervention would prevent troubled youth from turning to lives of crime. Judges could sentence offenders to prison or reform school. They could also place them on probation. Young offenders on probation did not go to prison. The court supervised them for a period of time. If they stayed out of trouble and did not commit any more crimes, the court released them from the system.

States, private charities, and religious groups built reform schools and industrial schools to educate and inspire troubled youth. Inmates often lived and worked in cottages, which were designed to look like homes. Substitute parents supervised them. Reform-school programs centered on education and work. Inmates made items such as nails, cheap shoes, or wicker chairs. The goal was to teach strong work habits so that the young prisoners could find jobs and earn a living after their release.

Julia Lathrop spent her career working for social reform on behalf of children, the disabled, and the mentally challenged.

As the nineteenth century came to a close, the number of prison inmates continued to climb. Convicts released from reformatories returned to prison as often as those released from penitentiaries. Scientists began to study criminal behavior. They looked for ways to treat criminals psychologically.

> The object of the prison discipline
> should be to produce
> not good prisoners
> but good citizens.
>
> —PRISON REFORMER THOMAS MOTT OSBORNE, 1921

CHAPTER FOUR

THE PROGRESSIVE ERA

In the early years of the twentieth century, U.S. cities grew dramatically. Millions of immigrants from eastern and southern Europe crowded into run-down tenements in city slums. They often worked in factories for low pay. This urban growth and poverty led to social problems. There was an increase in crime. Progressive reformers believed that poor living conditions and the social environment caused crime.

During the Progressive Era (1900–1920), social reform was at a peak in U.S. history. Reformers believed they could solve the nation's social, economic, and moral problems, and they believed this would end crime. It was a time of optimism. Many experts saw criminality as a biological problem. Some people, they believed, committed crimes because of their genetic makeup. According to Indiana's official policy, "Heredity plays a most important part in the transmission of crime, idiocy, and imbecility." In 1907 Indiana became the first state to pass a forced sterilization law. Leaders believed that sterilizing criminals, preventing them from having children, would weed out so-called defective people. The law allowed doctors to sterilize "confirmed criminals, idiots, rapists and imbeciles" in state institutions for whom "procreation [having children] is inadvisable." In this way, experts believed that criminals would not pass along their so-called defective natures to the next generation.

Several states passed similar forced sterilization laws. These laws remained in effect until 1942. That year the U.S. Supreme Court ruled against sterilizing criminals. The judges based their decision on the Equal Protection Clause of the Fourteenth Amendment to the Constitution. The Court ruled that, under this clause, certain prisoners were being unfairly singled out for sterilization. This was because the laws only applied to certain categories of crimes. Even after the ruling, however, the practice continued on a limited basis until the 1970s. Public pressure finally forced prisons to end the practice.

THE SCIENCE OF CRIMINOLOGY

Progressive reformers believed in a scientific solution to crime. They felt that people committed crimes because they were psychologically or emotionally sick. Just as physicians could diagnose and cure ailments of the body, psychologists and social workers should be able to diagnose and cure ailments of the mind. They thought this would stop antisocial behavior. According to this medical model, psychologists could identify the psychological factors that contributed to criminal behavior. Then they could design treatment programs to cure each offender. Scientists also began to measure rates of recidivism (committing other crimes after release from prison).

MORE LAWS AND LAW ENFORCERS

Reformers believed that the solution to crime was within reach. They were certain that if the U.S. government solved the nation's social problems, crime would disappear. As a result of this viewpoint, the government began to take a stronger role in law enforcement. In 1908, for example, President Theodore Roosevelt created the Federal Bureau of Investigation (FBI). The FBI investigated federal crimes, or crimes that crossed state lines.

Reformers thought new laws would force people to be good. They pressured Congress to pass laws against vice (immorality). Newspapers and magazines at this time wrote articles about "white slavery." They reported that young girls were being kidnapped and sold into prostitution. Reformers fought to end this practice. In 1910 Congress passed the Mann Act. This law made it a federal crime to take women across state lines for prostitution or any other immoral purpose. Next, reformers tried to cure addiction to heroin, opium, and morphine. In 1914 Congress passed the Harrison Narcotic Act. The law made it illegal to sell drugs without a prescription from a medical doctor.

Finally, reformers set their sights on alcoholism. They saw that alcohol abuse led to many crimes. Many people campaigned to ban alcohol. As a result of their efforts, the Eighteenth Amendment to the Constitution—known as Prohibition—went into effect in 1920. The amendment made it illegal to make, transport, or sell alcoholic beverages. With these new laws, progressives believed the federal government could rid the country of prostitution and the abuse of drugs and alcohol.

A federal police officer destroys barrels of illegal rum during Prohibition. Prohibition was in force in the United States from 1920 until 1933.

CORNERSTONES OF THE PROGRESSIVE ERA

During the Progressive Era, probation, parole, and indeterminate sentences became standard practice. The goal was to treat each criminal as an individual. The length of an offender's sentence depended on his or her response to treatment. Parole boards were established around the country. They decided when a prisoner was "cured" and ready for release from prison. Inmates who followed the rules served shorter sentences. Troublemakers served longer prison terms. Parole was designed to supervise and guide inmates after they left prison. It was meant to support the convict and help that person blend back into the community. Reformers also looked for other punishments for lawbreakers. Probation (supervision of offenders instead of prison time) was used for adults who committed minor crimes as well as for juveniles.

From the start, however, there were too many convicts on probation and parole. Parole officers could not keep up with all the people they had to monitor. Supervision was often limited to a list of dos and don'ts. "You are not to buy or drink alcoholic beverages," "work steady," and "obey all laws and conduct yourself as a good citizen." Convicts on parole rarely even saw their parole officers.

PRISON LIFE

As state and federal prison populations grew, several new prisons were built. Most followed the Auburn design. They were built with many tiers of small cells, each for a single inmate. But overcrowding forced two, three, and sometimes four prisoners to a cell. This overcrowding led to an increase

A kidnapper testifies before his parole board during the 1930s. Parole gained popularity during the Progressive Era but was poorly enforced. The program suffered from a shortage of parole officers.

in prison violence. All across the country, inmates attacked other inmates and their guards. Overcrowding also increased the spread of contagious diseases. Many prisoners died from tuberculosis, a lung disease for which there was no cure at the time.

Progressive reformers worked to improve conditions inside prisons. Some institutions hired psychologists to examine inmates, classify them, and recommend housing and work assignments. Some put new educational programs into place. But these efforts did little to change everyday life inside most prisons. There was not enough trained staff to create individualized treatment programs. So, inmates all followed the same daily routine. They were still locked in cages. Little of what they learned prepared them for life outside of prison.

Life was boring inside prisons of the Progressive Era. With limits on convict labor—and no safe alternatives for physical work—prisoners sat idle in a barren world of concrete and steel. According to prisoner Isidore Zimmerman, "The years pass; and in the drab gray world I inhabit nothing changes but the dates on the calendar. I sit in my cell and try one night, after lights out, to establish the chronology of all my wasted years."

PRISON WRITINGS

Inmates like Zimmerman added firsthand information to the prison reform movement. Many of them wrote about their experiences behind bars. Socialist Kate O'Hare was sent to prison for giving speeches against U.S. participation in World War I (1914–1918). She described the state penitentiary of Missouri where she served her sentence:

> Rats, flies, and cockroaches, not to mention other vermin unmentionable in polite society, were plagues of our prison life. The rats were perhaps worst of all. They overran the place in swarms, scampered over the dining tables, nibbled our bread, played in our dishes, crept into bed with us, chewed up our shoes, and carried off everything not nailed down or hung far above their reach.

Prison expert Frank Tannenbaum toured the United States in 1920. He inspected prisons all around the country. Tannenbaum wrote about his findings in great detail. His books shed light on the abuses that were still common practice in most prisons. Tannenbaum found many examples of physical punishments to discipline inmates. For example, "Thomas Shultz, boy of twenty-one years old, seven months after being sent from the insane asylum, was given 181 lashes and kept in the dungeon during the period of the flogging for nine days and fed on bread and water."

Tannenbaum thought all prisons should be abolished. "We must destroy the prison, root and branch," he wrote. "Let us substitute something. Almost anything will be an improvement. It cannot be worse. It cannot be more brutal and more useless. A farm, a school, a hospital, a factory, a playground—almost anything different will be better."

THOMAS MOTT OSBORNE

Retired businessman and former mayor of Auburn, New York, Thomas Mott Osborne was committed to prison reform. He volunteered to spend a week in Auburn Prison as inmate Thomas Brown. Osborne did this so that he could truly understand prison life. He found the prison brutal and barbaric. He wrote, "A prison should be a place of punishment, but not a torture chamber; a healing hospital, but not a madhouse."

Osborne felt prison made inmates worse instead of better, more a threat to society than they were when they entered prison. He described prisoners as men of honor and talent. "If you trust them they will show themselves worthy of trust," he wrote. "If you place responsibility upon them they will rise to it."

Shortly before Prohibition went into effect, Osborne became warden of Sing Sing Prison in New York. He immediately began to put his reform ideas into effect. His goal for the prison was to help the inmates gain self-respect. He also wanted the convicts to learn responsibility.

"Instead of confinement and repression in our prisons we must have the largest possible measure of individual freedom," he said. "Outside the walls a man must choose between work and idleness, between honesty and crime. Why not let him teach himself these lessons before he comes out?"

Osborne established the Mutual Welfare League at Sing Sing. The league allowed prisoners to govern themselves. It was designed to mirror, as much as possible, community life outside prison. This would prepare inmates for reentry into society. Inmates supervised one another and held their own disciplinary hearings. Their goal was, "To promote in every way the true interests and welfare of the men confined in prison." Their motto was, "Do Good—Make Good."

Thomas Mott Osborne *(right)* stands in the halls of Sing Sing in New York during his time as warden there.

Osborne's system seemed to work for a while. Violence inside the prison decreased. Escapes were less common, and recidivism rates for released prisoners dropped as well. But many people opposed Osborne's methods. They viewed prisoner self-government as a way of coddling convicts. They felt that the prison had lost its terror and become a "joy palace." If criminals were no longer afraid of prison, they reasoned, "crime would increase, life and property would be endangered, and public morals would suffer." Osborne was forced to resign after only two years as warden. Many of his reforms at Sing Sing were reversed.

UNREALIZED DREAMS

The high ideals of the Progressive Era fell short of their goals. Criminals were not "cured," and crime was not eliminated. But over the next decade, the reformers' efforts resulted in several improvements to prison conditions. Prisons became cleaner. They had larger libraries and organized sports. Most institutions relaxed the strict discipline and rules of silence. Lockstep marching and striped uniforms also disappeared from most prisons.

> The tougher you are in prison
> the more you are held in respect by
> the average prisoner.
>
> —PRISONER VICTOR F. NELSON, 1932

CHAPTER FIVE

THE BIG HOUSE

The Progressive Era's plan to wipe out prostitution, drugs, and alcohol backfired. Americans wanted their alcohol—illegal or not. There were plenty of people willing to provide it. During Prohibition organized crime controlled a multimillion dollar illegal business. They made bootleg liquor and smuggled it from state to state or from Canada. Police officers allowed the system to flourish. Many of them stuffed their pockets with bribes and looked the other way. As a result, historians call the decade of Prohibition the lawless decade.

CELEBRITY CROOKS

Crime was a top political issue in the 1920s and 1930s. Newspapers, radio programs, and movies made the lives of criminals seem glamorous. According to historian Frank Prassel, the "concentration of famous fugitives and their infamous crimes has no equal in the nation's history." The public read about gruesome murders such as the Saint Valentine's Day Massacre in 1929. Newspapers around the country described the gory scene in Chicago, Illinois. Seven gangsters were found riddled with machine gun bullets. No one was ever tried for the murders. Most people held mob leader Al Capone responsible.

The public also followed the reports on Bonnie and Clyde. The pair traveled around the country robbing banks. Some fans even swarmed the car where Bonnie and Clyde were killed by police officers. They took stray bullets, bits of clothing, and locks of Bonnie's hair as souvenirs. "Public enemies" such as John Dillinger, Pretty Boy Floyd, Machine Gun Kelly, Baby Face Nelson, and Al Capone became household names. According to a female convict of the era:

> Gangsters? They were grown as naturally in the alleys and gutters of our slum neighborhood as mosquitoes grow in a swamp. Now when I pick up a paper and read of one more noble crusade against gangsters, I smile—and understand. To whip up a crusade against gangsters is as ludicrous as to organize an army of mosquito-swatters while the swamplands where they multiply are left untouched. Society makes gunmen and then gets excited when their guns go off.

THE GREAT DEPRESSION

Public awareness of crime increased and so did fear. The stock market crash of 1929 added to the

Al Capone winks at the camera during a break from his trial for tax evasion in 1932. During the 1930s, the United States had a wave of celebrity criminals.

general anxiety and led to the Great Depression (1929–1942). Thousands of workers suddenly found themselves unable to get jobs. Between one-quarter and one-third of Americans were out of work. In some cities, the unemployment rate reached 50 percent.

The nation struggled through the economic hardships of the Depression. More and more families found themselves without shoes, without clothes, without homes, and without food. Some ate weeds or sifted through garbage cans. Others stood in relief lines for hours, hoping for a bowl of soup or a crust of bread. Previously law-abiding citizens stole food to feed their families.

The number of people in prison increased. Inmates sat in cells packed to overflowing. Cheap, prison-made goods sold for lower prices than goods made outside of prison. Law-abiding Americans, hungry and out of work, thought this was unfair. They felt that prisoners should not be employed when they, good citizens, could not find work. In response, Congress passed the Hawes-Cooper Act. This law allowed any state to ban the sale of prison-made goods made in another state. Many states also passed laws to restrict prison-made goods from being sold on the open market. As a result, the majority of prisoners had no work to pass the time.

CRIME AS A NATIONAL PROBLEM

Until the 1930s, each state had dealt with the crime within its borders. During Prohibition, crime control began to shift from a state to a national concern. President Herbert Hoover (who served from 1929 until 1933) formed a committee to study all aspects of the criminal justice system. Former attorney general George Wickersham led the group. In 1931 the committee published its findings. The fourteen-volume report covered Prohibition enforcement, police behavior, and the state of U.S. prisons.

Volume nine, *The Report on Penal Institutions, Probation and Parole*, described the miserable conditions inside most prisons. It showed the discontent of inmates. "The present prison system is antiquated [out of date] and inefficient," stated the report. "It does not reform the criminal. It fails to protect society. There is reason to believe that it contributes to the increase of crime by hardening the prisoner." The report stated that prison did little to prepare an inmate for life outside prison as a law-abiding citizen. It recommended classifying prisoners based on their backgrounds, personalities, and crimes. This would relieve prison overcrowding and eliminate discipline problems. Only the most dangerous criminals would be sent to high security prisons. All other offenders would be housed in simple, inexpensive buildings with less security. The committee suggested prisons develop education and labor programs to promote inmate self-respect. They also wanted to increase the use of probation and parole.

There were several positive results from the Wickersham report. It became standard practice to classify prisoners according to their crimes. This led to the development of maximum and minimum security prisons for men. Maximum security prisons were for hard-core criminals. They held inmates who were convicted of the most serious crimes. Minimum

Prisoners at the New York State Reformatory, a minimum security prison, take a plumbing class in the 1920s.

security prisons held inmates who were good candidates for rehabilitation. They had less supervision than inmates in maximum security prisons. They also had more privileges. In addition, separate prisons for women and juvenile offenders gained wider support as a result of the report.

WAR ON CRIME

During this period, the U.S. government declared war on crime. The FBI was expanded under the leadership of its powerful director, J. Edgar Hoover. Congress passed several new federal laws to respond to certain crimes. For example, Charles Lindbergh, the first person to fly solo across the Atlantic Ocean, became the victim of the "crime of the century." His two-year-old son was kidnapped and murdered in 1932. Later that year, Congress passed the Lindbergh Law. The law made kidnapping a federal crime. Other new laws made it a federal crime to rob a national bank, transport stolen goods valued at five thousand dollars or more across state lines, or drive a stolen car across state lines.

THE ROCK

As a result of these new laws, the number of federal crimes increased in the 1900s. The government built several new federal prisons to handle the surge of prisoners. The Federal Bureau of Prisons was formed to supervise these prisons. In 1934 the bureau converted Alcatraz, an army prison, to a federal prison. Alcatraz was known as the Rock because it sat on a jagged, rocky island off the coast of San Francisco, California. The prison was considered escape-proof. One mile (1.6 km) of dangerous ocean tides kept prisoners from attempting to swim away from the fortress prison.

Alcatraz was considered the prison of last resort. The most hardened criminals were handpicked from other prisons and sent to Alcatraz. They were the men prison officials felt could not be rehabilitated. Attorney General Homer Cummings explained, "Here may be isolated the criminals of the vicious and irredeemable type so that their evil influence may not be extended to other prisoners who are disposed to rehabilitate themselves." Al Capone and Machine Gun Kelly were two of the famous residents of Alcatraz.

Alcatraz was a maximum security, minimum privilege prison. Inmates were given food, clothing, shelter, and medical attention. Everything else was a privilege. Prisoners had to earn the chance to work. They also had to earn the right to borrow books from the prison library or to use the exercise yard. Until they earned it, inmates had no contact with the outside world. "It is the 'island of mistreated men,'" said inmate Al Loomis. "Soon it will be the 'island of mad men.'"

THE BIG HOUSE

Although the federal prison system was growing, the majority of convicts were still housed in state prisons. A new type of state maximum security prison, known as the Big House, was developed in the 1920s and 1930s. Each one held an average of twenty-five hundred inmates. Stateville Penitentiary, located approximately 30 miles (48 km) southwest of Chicago, was Illinois's largest Big House. It was built in a circular design. Four round cell houses, called roundhouses, each contained four tiers of cells. Each cell had a window and a toilet. Armed guards stood in a tower in the center of the round-house. A guard standing in the tower could, by rotating 360 degrees, see into every cell. Stateville was home to some of Chicago's most notorious gangsters and murderers.

A roundhouse at Stateville Penitentiary in Illinois

Powerful gangs dominated the prison. Carried over from the streets, ethnic-based crime groups kept their loyalties inside the prison walls. A status system ruled among inmates based on the crimes for which they had been convicted. Murderers and robbers held the highest status. Sex offenders held the lowest. The "rat," an inmate who snitched to the guards about other inmates, was universally despised. The "right guy," a convict who minded his own business and was loyal to the other cons, was admired. Prison guards often gave high-status inmates special privileges. In exchange, these inmates helped the guards maintain order. As a result of this system, prison rackets flourished. Food, cigarettes, alcohol, drugs, and information were available for a price. According to one Stateville inmate, "We were gambling, drinkin'. . . . There were gangs of prisoners runnin' wild all over the yard. . . . The big-shot cons didn't have to make the count [stand in their cells to be counted] . . . didn't have to work if they didn't feel like it. They ran the place."

Gangs kept their power through violence against other gangs or guards. Knifings, fistfights, and assaults broke out daily throughout the prison system. Inmate Bill Sands described the prison violence in the Big House at San Quentin, California:

> Everywhere, every minute—like the air you breathe—there is the threat of violence lurking beneath the surface. Unlike the air, it is heavy, massive, as oppressive as molasses. It permeates [spreads through] every second of everyone's existence—the potential threat of sudden, ferocious annihilation. It is as grey and swift and unpredictable as a shark and just as unvocal. There is no letup from it—ever.

ATTICA

In the early 1930s, Attica Prison opened in a tiny village in western New York. At the time, it was the most expensive prison ever built. Attica was designed to be a humane prison. It would be the most modern prison in the country. According to the *New York Times*, Attica would have, "beds with springs and mattresses, a cafeteria with food under glass, recreation rooms. . . . Sunlight will stream into cells and every prisoner will have an individual radio."

When the first inmates arrived at Attica, however, they found a dreary fortress of brick and steel. A 30-foot-high wall (9 m) surrounded the prison. The weak economy of the Depression had made it impossible to put in place all the builder's plans. For this reason, life in Attica was like life in other prisons around the country. One long-term prisoner compared his life in a prison cell to the animals he saw caged in a zoo:

> Visiting the zoo as a child, I'd been struck by the way a lion—pacing then as I was pacing now—would progressively shorten the distance covered each time, anticipating the presence of the bars before he reached them, anticipating the need to turn and turning a step sooner, then two steps, then three, until finally he was no longer pacing but turning on himself, revolving on his own axis.

PRISON RIOTS

During the early years of the Depression, riots broke out in prisons all across the country. Overcrowding, boredom, and poor living conditions were blamed. At California's Folsom Prison, two officers and nine inmates were killed before order was restored. In Clinton, New York, three inmates died in a prison riot. Auburn Prison exploded when an inmate overpowered a guard and grabbed his keys. The prisoner passed out guns to several inmates and started a general riot. Four inmates escaped, six work areas were burned, and the prison was severely damaged. Eventually, guards with rifles, machine guns, and tear gas put down the riot. Similar violence took place in prisons in Illinois, Kansas, and Colorado.

THE DEATH PENALTY

In the 1930s, most Americans supported the use of the death penalty. Executions increased as the ultimate punishment for crime. The South had the highest death penalty rates.

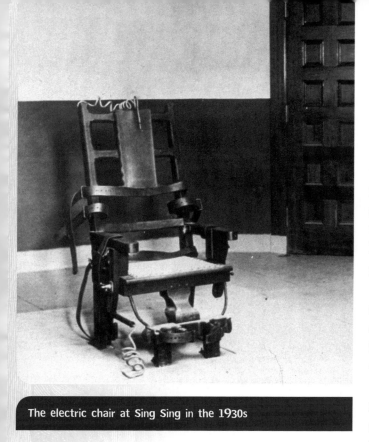

The electric chair at Sing Sing in the 1930s

Scientists of the time looked for quick and painless ways to kill convicted felons. Some convicts were electrocuted in electric chairs. Others were put to death by breathing poisonous gas in gas chambers. Modern executions were not public events, as they had been in colonial days. They took place in private, behind prison walls.

Because of racial discrimination, African Americans were arrested, tried, and sent to prison more often than whites. During the Depression, this situation got worse. On October 1, 1936, the *New York Times* reported, "Alabama's new Burglary Law was applied here for the first time today when a jury found James Thomas, Negro, guilty of burglary in which $1.50 was the loot and fixed his punishment at life imprisonment. The jurors had heard a strong plea from the prosecutor for the death penalty."

NEW CHALLENGES

Prohibition ended and the United States struggled out of the Depression. The 1930s came to a close, and the world moved toward World War II (1939–1945). The United States faced a new set of challenges in dealing with people who broke the law.

> The treatment of prisoners should
> emphasize not their exclusion
> from the community,
> but their continuing part in it.
>
> —UNITED NATIONS, *STANDARD MINIMUM RULES
> FOR THE TREATMENT OF PRISONERS*, 1955

CHAPTER SIX

THE CORRECTIONS ERA

In 1939 German dictator Adolf Hitler invaded Poland. Hitler's goal was to dominate the world. Under his leadership, Germany quickly invaded and took over Denmark, Norway, the Netherlands, Belgium, and France. U.S. president Franklin Delano Roosevelt (FDR) and the U.S. government opposed Hitler. But most Americans didn't want to send U.S. troops into a foreign war. Then, on December 7, 1941, Japan attacked the U.S. naval base at Pearl Harbor, Hawaii. The surprise attack killed more than two thousand U.S. citizens. It also damaged or destroyed eight U.S. battleships. The next day, the United States declared war on Japan, Germany, and their allies.

All American men between the ages of eighteen and forty-five had to register for the draft. At that time, the draft was a federal lottery system that chose men for the military by random numbers. This ruling included prison inmates. Many convicts wanted to join the armed forces. The army judged inmates on an individual basis. Those who had been convicted of serious crimes, such as murder, kidnapping, or rape, were not allowed to serve. The Department of Corrections released its control of drafted inmates. They were placed under the authority of the U.S. Army. During World War II, the prison population dropped. Most of the pool of potential offenders was drafted.

HELPING THE WAR EFFORT

Americans were full of patriotism during the war. Everyone wanted to aid the war effort. Inmates who could not enlist helped in other ways. Many of them donated blood for the Red Cross. To help the soldiers fighting in the Pacific, some convicts volunteered to take part in malaria research. They agreed to be bitten by malaria-bearing mosquitoes so that researchers could test drugs to treat malaria. This disease was common in the hot regions of Asia where many soldiers were fighting. Prisoner Nathan Leopold wrote about the malaria research in which he took part:

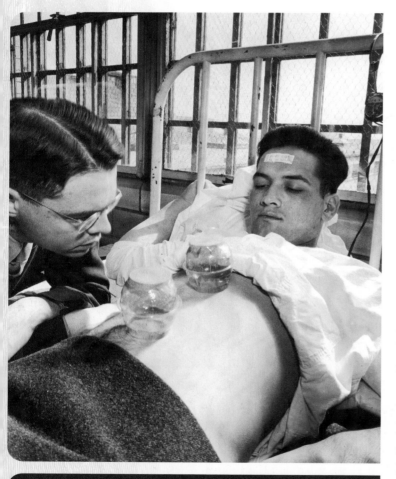

An army doctor administers a malaria test on a convict at the Stateville Penitentiary in Illinois in 1945.

Being present at the very birth of new knowledge is a privilege given to few people in this world. And many of us were not unmindful of the fact that for the first time in a long, long time, we were being offered the opportunity of doing something which would be appreciated by society; something that would make people feel less harsh toward convicts, and cause people to remember that we, too, were human.

In prisons all across the country, inmates made supplies that were needed for the war effort. They made shoes, shirts, overalls, and trousers for soldiers. They made army mattresses, blankets, and wooden bunks. Prisoners also made racks to hold bombs, bomb steering fins, and aircraft engines.

J. EDGAR HOOVER AND THE FBI

The FBI expanded its focus during World War II. It began to track down spies. As a result, the number of FBI agents increased during the war years. After the United States and its allies won the war, the FBI grew even more. FBI agents were needed for the Cold War (1945–1991)—to keep track of the actions of the Soviet Union in its drive to spread Communism around the world.

In 1950 the FBI introduced a publicity campaign to help catch criminals. The "Ten Most Wanted" list gave the names, descriptions, and photographs of the criminals the FBI most wanted to track down. The agency encouraged citizens to help them search for these dangerous criminals. Americans were told to contact the FBI with information about any of the people on the list.

Organized crime families, such as those of the Mafia, attracted a lot of attention in the press. In November 1957, FBI director J. Edgar Hoover began the "Top Hoodlum" program. Hoover started the program to show that the FBI was fighting organized crime. Each FBI field office had to identify the ten major mob members, or hoodlums, in their area. Once the criminals were identified, the field office closely watched them. Agents prepared reports on their activities. In this way, the FBI learned a great deal about the inner workings of organized crime. However, few convictions resulted from the program.

PRISON RIOTS

The crime rate rose in the 1950s, and the prison population grew. Prison riots became more common. The problems in these prisons were the same problems that had plagued prisons of earlier times. Inmates blamed overcrowding, poor food, boredom, and lack of adequate medical care for the riots. They held brutal guards responsible for pushing them into violence. At Trenton Prison in New Jersey, sixty-nine prisoners took over the prison print shop. They blocked the doors and held two guards and two shop instructors hostage. Then they destroyed the shop. After three days of negotiations, prison officials agreed to inspect the prison. They also agreed to allow the inmates to form a grievance committee to discuss their complaints.

In the prison at Jackson, Michigan, inmates destroyed property, took hostages, and tore up the prison grounds. Groups of convicts freed their fellow inmates. They broke windows and ripped out toilet bowls. The freed prisoners stood ankle-deep in toilet water, broken glass, and wreckage.

The Michigan rioters gave prison officials a list of demands. They wanted better medical treatment, more access to counselors, and an inmate council. Similar revolts broke out in prisons all across the country. James V. Bennett, director of the Federal Bureau of Prisons, believed that prisons had problems because experts were confused about their purpose. He wrote:

> On the one hand, prisons are expected to punish; on the other, they are supposed to reform. They are expected to discipline rigorously at the same time that they teach self-reliance. They are built to be operated like vast impersonal machines, yet they are expected to fit men to live normal community lives. . . . They refuse the prisoner a voice in self-government, but they expect him to become a thinking citizen in a democratic society.

CLASSIFY, TREAT, AND REHABILITATE

Bennett and others defined the problem, but solutions were harder to pinpoint. Several committees were formed to study prison conditions, especially inside large prisons. Reform became a popular topic in the media and among politicians. Many states began to use diagnostic centers. At the diagnostic center, health-care professionals studied each convict's medical, psychological, and criminal history. They decided if the prisoner should be sent to a maximum, medium, or minimum security prison. The staff at the diagnostic center also designed a treatment plan for each offender. Convict Malcolm Braly wrote about the classification system from a prisoner's point of view:

> We quickly learned we were expected to view this journey through prison as a quest, and the object of our quest was to discover our problem. It was assumed we were here because of psychological problems, and our task now, by which we could expect to be judged, was to isolate and come to terms with them. . . . You were willing to concede [admit] you might have a problem even if you had to invent one on the spot.

In the 1950s, the American Prison Association changed its name to the American Correctional Association. Prisons were renamed correctional institutions. The new term was based on the idea that prisons were places where convicts were treated and their behavior "corrected." Guards were called correctional officers. Solitary confinement was renamed the adjustment center.

Correctional institutions worked to treat inmates, rather than simply house them. The goal was to change convicts' attitudes and behaviors. Since criminals were thought to be mentally disturbed, psychologists and counselors became a large part of the prison system. They worked to understand the mind of the criminal. These mental health experts looked at the factors that caused people to commit crimes. They also studied inmates and designed programs to help them control their antisocial behavior. Training for prison employees also increased during this period.

Prison officials tried to develop step-by-step plans for rehabilitation. To accomplish this goal, a variety of treatment programs were put in place. These programs expanded the rehabilitation methods of the Progressive Era. Counselors in correctional facilities began to use behavioral modification. This treatment plan tries to change behavior through rewards and punishments. Prisons also began to offer more individual and group counseling. They added new vocational (job) training and high school and college classes. Many prisons offered classes in business English, typing, and commercial art. Others expanded their athletic programs to include football, baseball, softball, and basketball. New prisons built during this period had windows, well-equipped libraries, and gyms. The Texas prison system began to host prison rodeos. Rodeo events included goat

Convicts participate in the annual Texas Prison Rodeo in Huntsville, Texas, in 1980. The Texas rodeo program lasted until 1986.

roping, bull riding, bronc riding, and wild horse racing. The popular show entertained inmates, employees, and the public.

People around the world began to focus on rehabilitation. In the mid-1950s, the United Nations (an international peacekeeping group) published the *Standard Minimum Rules for the Treatment of Prisoners*. The *Rules* included guidelines for housing, food, medical services, and discipline in prisons. They stated that the purpose of treatment programs was to establish in prisoners, "the will to lead law-abiding and self-supporting lives after their release and to fit them to do so."

JUVENILE DELINQUENTS

Juvenile crime increased in the 1950s. As a result, more children were sent to reform schools. According to statistics from the U.S. Department of Justice Juvenile Court, the delinquency level was 56 percent higher in the mid-1950s than in the late 1940s. Many people blamed the rise in juvenile delinquency on the influence of mass media. In the postwar economic boom, teens had their own money for music, movies, clothing, and comic books. More teens used drugs and belonged to gangs.

At the time, many adults thought children became delinquents because they did not have a proper education. Others thought it was because they came from poorly functioning families. Many experts believed the way to stop juvenile crime was to create a Youth Correction Authority. Several states created this agency. This group of psychologists and social workers decided how to deal with young lawbreakers. The Youth Correction Authority matched each offender's individual needs to the treatment program best suited to meet those needs. The goal was to give each offender the greatest chance for rehabilitation.

In practice, professionals found it difficult to scientifically diagnose offenders. The factors that led to juvenile delinquency were too complex to fit into neat diagnostic tests. Also, not enough specialized treatment programs were available to meet the growing need.

A MURDER SPARKS THE FIGHT FOR CIVIL RIGHTS

In the mid-1950s, the Supreme Court ruled that separate public schools for black children and white children were unfair. Separate schools denied black children the same opportunity as white children to get a good education. The landmark decision was known as *Brown v. Board of Education*. It ended segregation in public schools. The ruling paved the way for integration, one of the key goals of the modern civil rights movement. Many southern whites fought against the new freedoms granted African Americans. Violence against blacks, especially in the South, increased as black children began to attend white schools. Racial tension and violence broke out in cities all across the country, both inside and outside of prison.

Rates of imprisonment among African Americans increased in the 1950s. In part, this was linked to an unwritten double standard in the criminal justice system. The system, especially in the South, operated differently for whites than for blacks. White offenders were not convicted for crimes against African Americans as often as African Americans were convicted for crimes against whites.

A shocking case in Mississippi illustrated this difference. Emmett Till, a fourteen-year-old African American boy, was accused of whistling at a white woman. The woman's husband and his half brother kidnapped, tortured, and murdered Emmett. They tied a heavy weight around his body and dumped him into a local river. The men admitted they snatched Emmett from his bed in the middle of the night. They were brought to trial and found not guilty by an all-white jury of men. The jury reached their decision after discussing the case for only one hour and eight minutes. "If we hadn't stopped to drink pop, it wouldn't have taken that long," said one of the jurors. A few months after the trial, the two men confessed to the murder in *Look* magazine. The crime and trial caused an international uproar. African Americans and many other people grew fearful and angry. They saw that the criminal justice system in the United States was unfair.

The all-white jury *(above, seated)* in the Emmett Till murder trial of the 1950s found the two white defendants not guilty. Only months later, the two men confessed to Till's murder. The crime and its aftermath inflamed the black community and its supporters.

BLACK MUSLIMS

In the 1950s, a group called the Nation of Islam grew in influence in the black neighborhoods of some U.S. inner cities. Known as the Black Muslims, this group was an offshoot of the Islamic religion. Many poor African Americans were drawn to the Black Muslims. The group wanted to form a separate black nation, in which African Americans would be free from racial discrimination and could govern their own affairs. As a college student in Atlanta, Georgia, explained, "For the man who is not white, Islam is the hope for justice and equality in the world we must build tomorrow."

The ideals of the Black Muslims appealed to many African Americans in prison. Members were taught to work hard and to avoid drugs and alcohol. Prisoner Malcolm Little joined the Black Muslims while in prison in Massachusetts. After his conversion, he spent the long days of his sentence for burglary reading in the prison library. He copied and studied pages from a dictionary to improve his vocabulary and handwriting. Little took

Malcolm X, a former convict, inspired many people to fight for their civil rights.

the name Malcolm X. After his release from prison, he became an influential civil rights leader.

According to author, social activist, and fellow inmate Eldridge Cleaver, "Malcolm X had a special meaning for black convicts. A former prisoner himself, he had risen from the lowest depths to great heights. For this reason he was a symbol of hope, a model for thousands of black convicts who found themselves trapped in the vicious PPP cycle: prison-parole-prison."

As membership in the Nation of Islam increased, so did the number of Black Muslims in prison. As Muslims, they demanded pork-free meals. Muslims are not permitted to eat pork. They also demanded temples and their own ministers for worship. They sued for the right to wear traditional Muslim clothing and religious medals. Several courts ruled that the inmates were not being granted their First Amendment right to practice the religion of their choice. Those rulings paved the way for a full-blown prisoner rights movement in the 1960s.

INTO THE '60S

In spite of the widely held belief that individualized treatment programs would permanently change inmate behavior, recidivism rates remained high. Released prisoners continued to commit crimes. A fierce debate sprang up among criminal justice experts. Some argued that the programs were valid but the lack of trained staff made success impossible. Others said that rehabilitation simply did not work. Eventually, the radical changes of the 1960s found their way into U.S. prisons. This brought a major shift in thinking about crime and punishment.

> The real horror of prison is not
> the torment of human flesh,
> but the system that tolerates it.
>
> —ATTICA INMATE JEROME WASHINGTON, 1981

CHAPTER SEVEN

A FIGHT FOR RIGHTS

The 1960s were a time of social unrest. The Vietnam War (1957–1975) was raging, with no end in sight. Young American men were drafted to serve in this war. As the war continued and the death toll rose, American support for the war dropped. Many Americans wanted to end the draft and U.S. involvement in Vietnam. In 1963 the young, charismatic president John F. Kennedy was assassinated. Two years later, civil rights leader Malcolm X was murdered. In 1968 civil rights leader Dr. Martin Luther King Jr. and presidential candidate Robert F. Kennedy were also gunned down. The murders of these influential leaders, symbols of hope for the nation, set off a period of intense turmoil in the United States. The decade saw civil rights movements, antiwar protests, race riots, and activism among college students. Change was the buzz-word of the day. African Americans, other minority groups, and women demanded their rights.

CRIMINAL JUSTICE GOES PRO

During the 1960s, colleges and universities increased the number of criminal justice degree programs for students. These programs trained police officers and other law enforcement workers. The U.S. government studied the environmental factors that caused crime. They tried to figure out how to prevent it. An expert in corrections, Vincent O'Leary, professor of criminal justice in Albany, New York, wrote, "There are definite subcultures in our society in which violence exists, in which violence is a way of life. . . . If you are really going to change things, you are going to have to change, not just the man, but the whole of that violent subculture of which he is a part." The government attempted to change the subculture that bred crime through new laws designed to end poverty and racial injustice.

THE RIGHTS OF THE ACCUSED

In the 1960s, reformers worked to make the criminal justice system more humane. The focus shifted to increasing the civil rights of people accused of crimes. Several new laws were passed to make sure the constitutional rights of accused and convicted offenders were not ignored by the criminal justice system. One important new law placed restrictions on police officers who questioned suspects.

On March 13, 1963, Ernesto Miranda was arrested at his home. He was taken to a Phoenix, Arizona, police station. At the police station, the victim he was accused of kidnapping and raping identified him. Miranda was then taken to a room for questioning. The police officers who interviewed him did not tell Miranda that he had the right to have an attorney present. They did not tell him that anything he said could be used against him in court. Miranda wrote out a confession two hours later.

Miranda was found guilty and sentenced to twenty to thirty years in prison. His lawyers appealed the conviction, and the case went all the way to the U.S. Supreme Court. In 1966 the Court agreed with Miranda's lawyers. They had argued that Miranda had been denied his constitutional rights. Police officers had not told him that he could have a lawyer present at his questioning. The court overturned Miranda's conviction. This ruling resulted in the Miranda Law. The law requires police officers to inform suspects of their rights before questioning:

> You have the right to remain silent. If you give up the right to remain silent, anything you say can and will be used against you in a court of law. You have the right to an attorney. If you desire an attorney and cannot afford one, an attorney will be obtained for you before police questioning.

Ernesto Miranda *(right)* speaks with his attorney *(left)* during his second trial in 1967. The appeal of Miranda's first conviction led to the requirement that police officers inform suspects of their rights before they question them.

Ernesto Miranda was later convicted in a new trial. Witnesses testified against him, and enough evidence was presented to convince a jury of his guilt.

Not everyone was happy about the new focus on the rights of the accused. J. Edgar Hoover, director of the FBI, strongly criticized the courts. "We mollycoddle [pamper] young criminals and release unreformed hoodlums to prey anew on society," he said. "The bleeding hearts [sentimental people], particularly among the judiciary, are so concerned for young criminals that they become indifferent to the rights of law-abiding citizens."

PRISONER RIGHTS

The civil rights movement spread to U.S. prisons. In 1964 the Supreme Court established the principle that prisoners have constitutional rights. Inmates demanded the ability to exercise those rights. Their appeals affected every aspect of prison life. They fought for better living conditions and religious freedom. They wanted to be able to receive books and magazines. They also wanted to be able to write letters to people outside of prison.

Discipline inside prisons changed as well. Inmates used the ban on "cruel and unusual punishment" of the Eighth Amendment to the Constitution to bring about the changes. Prison guards had to stop all forms of corporal punishment. Inmates accused of breaking prison rules were allowed to hear the charges against them. They could present evidence and witnesses at disciplinary hearings. Prisoners could no longer be thrown into solitary confinement on the personal whim of a single guard.

Abuses still occurred inside prisons. However, the new rulings established the idea that prison conditions had to live up to minimum legal standards outlined in the Constitution. In addition to disciplinary hearings, prisoners were also allowed to file lawsuits and appeals related to their convictions. The Supreme Court ruled that prisoners were allowed, "a full and fair hearing" on every claim that their constitutional rights had been violated.

The country was deeply divided over these changes in the criminal justice system. Some Americans agreed with them. They felt the rulings were a crucial step toward removing long-standing injustice. Others thought the new laws weakened police authority and focused too much on the rights of the criminal rather than those of the victim.

THE PRESIDENT'S CRIME COMMISSION

In 1965 President Lyndon Johnson created the President's Crime Commission. The agency looked at the entire criminal justice system, including law enforcement, the courts, and prisons. It studied the impact of crime on U.S. society. According to President Johnson:

> Crime is a sore on the face of America. It is a menace on our streets. It is a drain on our cities. It is a corruptor of our youth. It is the cause of untold suffering and loss. But just saying this does not solve the problem that we have before us. We must bring it under control and then root out the cause. So let the nation know today that we have taken a pledge not only to reduce crime but to banish it.

The commission examined prisons, personnel, and programs. They tried to develop standard treatment methods for each type of offender. They wanted to expand probation and parole. The goal was to get offenders out of the criminal justice system as early as possible. The commission believed that one of its most important tasks was "the examination of what is being done to make sure that when the offender is discharged from prison he is not forced to resume his career in crime because no other career is open to him."

COMMUNITY CORRECTIONS

Criminal justice experts saw how difficult it was to rehabilitate inmates in prison. Longtime prisoner Jack Henry Abbott explained the problem in his book *In the Belly of the Beast*:

> I cannot adjust to daily life in prison. For almost twenty

years this has been true. I have never gone a month in prison without . . . disciplinary action for violating "rules." Not in all these years. Does this mean I must die in prison? Does this mean I cannot "adjust" to society outside prison? The government answers yes–but I *remember* society, and it is not like prison. I feel that if I ever did *adjust to prison*, I could by that alone never adjust to society.

Community corrections programs hoped to prepare inmates for life outside prison. Supervised parole and probation were common. Work-release programs became more available. These programs allowed prisoners to leave prison during daytime hours to work at jobs. Studies showed that recidivism rates were highest during the first few months after an inmate's release. Halfway houses were built to help inmates make the transition from prison back into society. The number of residents a halfway house could accept was limited. But halfway houses provided several important services to released convicts. Most halfway houses helped former inmates find jobs. They provided room and board, counseling, and recreation. Many people were against halfway houses, however, because the average citizen feared former convicts living in their neighborhoods.

In the spirit of prisoner rights, popular support for the death penalty sank to an all-time low in the late 1960s. The Eighth Amendment ban on cruel and unusual punishment was cited as proof that capital punishment should be abolished. "It is an act for which we should be deeply ashamed," said Joe Margulies, defense attorney for executed Texas prisoner Betty Beets. "It is an act of cowardice." In 1968, for the first time in U.S. history, not a single convict was executed.

CRIME AS A POLITICAL ISSUE

Serious crime, including murder and robbery, increased during the 1960s. By the late 1960s, most Americans saw crime as one of the nation's biggest problems. They pressured the government to do something about it. Crime control became a major campaign issue in the 1968 presidential election. Democratic governor George Wallace often talked about crime. He claimed that "if you walk out of this hotel tonight and someone knocks you on the head, *he'll* be out of jail before *you're* out of the hospital, and on Monday morning, they'll try the policeman instead of the criminal."

When Republican Richard Nixon won the presidency in 1968, he promised to get tough on crime. He wanted to change the direction of the Supreme Court. One of his first acts as president was to select Warren Burger to lead the Supreme Court. Burger was known to be a tough law-and-order judge.

THE STANFORD PRISON EXPERIMENT

In the summer of 1971, twenty-four intelligent, healthy, law-abiding college men at Stanford University agreed to take part in a study of human behavior in prison. The students were randomly selected to play the roles of prisoners or prison guards. The Stanford Prison Experiment was scheduled to run for two weeks. Researchers planned to track changes in the behavior of guards and prisoners.

The experiment had to be called off after only six days. The men playing prisoners showed signs of acute mental distress. The men playing prison guards behaved with extreme cruelty. Researchers were shocked at the profound changes in behavior in both the prisoners and the guards. Their findings showed that the prison setting caused inmates to feel angry, depressed, and hopeless. The prison environment also caused formerly good men, playing the role of guards, to abuse their prisoners.

The day after the Stanford Prison Experiment ended, a riot broke out at San Quentin Prison in California. Prisoner George Jackson had attempted to escape. Several guards and prisoners were killed. A few weeks later, New York's Attica Prison erupted in one of the worst prison riots in history.

ATTICA

On September 9, 1971, more than thirteen hundred inmates at Attica Prison took the guards hostage. They set fire to several buildings and controlled the prison for four days. The inmates wrote a declaration of beliefs to the American people:

> WE are MEN! We are not beasts and do not intend to be beaten or driven as such. The entire prison populace has set forth to change forever the ruthless brutalization and disregard for the lives of the prisoners here and throughout the United States.

The rioters demanded twenty-eight changes in prison policy. They wanted better medical care, better food, and more educational programs. News reporters recorded the drama as it unfolded. The nation watched the siege on television. On September 13, New York governor Nelson Rockefeller ordered state troopers to storm the prison and retake control. When the battle was over, forty-three people were dead. The death toll included eleven hostages.

Televising the Attica riot brought prison conditions into the living rooms of the American people. From the comfort of their homes, they saw a hidden world exposed. The effects were dramatic and long lasting. The

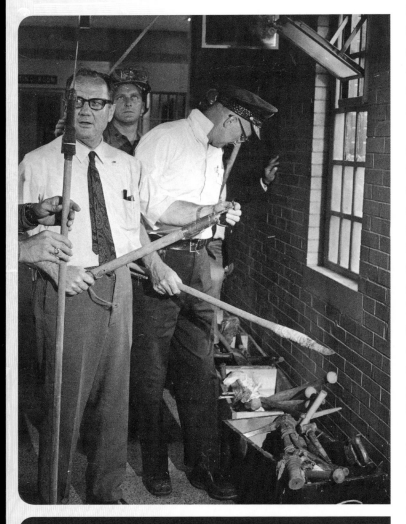

Attica Prison guards examine the weapons of inmates used during the deadly Attica riot in 1971.

riot and the publicity surrounding it triggered many legal battles. Inmates were charged with criminal actions during the siege. Prison guards were charged in a class action (group) lawsuit for brutality against inmates. The legal action lasted for years. As a result, the State of New York was forced to make several changes to its prisons. They installed new security measures and expanded programs for inmates.

A LANDMARK SUPREME COURT RULING

Throughout this period, many people questioned the legality of capital punishment. These legal challenges reached the Supreme Court in 1972. In a close decision, the Court found that African Americans, the poor, and other disadvantaged groups were executed more often than other groups. Because of this, the Court ruled in *Furman v. Georgia* that the death penalty was cruel and unusual punishment. It violated the Eighth Amendment and Fourteenth Amendment to the Constitution. With this Court ruling, more than six hundred prisoners on death row no longer faced the death penalty for their crimes. Almost immediately, some states began to write new death penalty laws. These new laws would allow capital punishment while sticking to the standards of fairness set forth by the Supreme Court.

The violence at Attica Prison and the rising crime rate convinced many Americans that the criminal justice system was not working. Confidence in the system fell to an all-time low. Fear and anxiety over crime crept into U.S. homes. The mood of the country grew more punitive toward criminals. Most people believed that if criminals were punished more severely, crime would decrease. It was the end of the era of optimistic criminal justice reform and the beginning of a conservative get-tough policy on crime.

> **Don't do the crime,**
> **if you can't do the time.**
>
> —POPULAR SAYING OF THE CRIMINAL JUSTICE SYSTEM, 1970S

CHAPTER EIGHT

GETTING TOUGH

In the late 1960s and early 1970s, criminal justice expert Robert Martinson and a team of researchers studied rehabilitation programs in prisons. They gathered information from prisons in the United States and around the world. Their goal was to find out which programs worked to rehabilitate convicts. They measured how many released inmates committed additional crimes. Martinson studied education and job training, social-skill development training, and the effects of counseling. In 1974 he published his findings in a massive fourteen-hundred-page report. The report bluntly stated that rehabilitation did not work. Released prisoners continued to commit crimes. The public reduced the findings of the report to the phrase, "nothing works."

In the late 1970s and early 1980s, the U.S. economy sagged. The nation faced a deep recession (a slowdown of business activity and new jobs). Nightly news reports of gruesome murders, serial killers, school shootings, and global terrorism fueled a general sense of unease. The public's fear of crime increased. Cries for law and order grew louder and louder. This led to a tough-on-crime trend. Lawmakers responded to the voters in their districts by passing harsh new sentencing laws. They hired more police officers, built more prisons, and kept convicts in prison for longer periods of time.

TOUGHER SENTENCES

Many Americans thought the criminal justice system was too lenient. The Martinson report seemed to prove that prisons did not change criminals for the better. For this reason, many people felt that offenders should be locked up for long periods of time. That way, they could not harm society. Indeterminate sentences and parole were criticized because they allowed dangerous criminals to be released from prison. High-profile crimes, such as the murder of basketball superstar Michael Jordan's father by two men on parole, reinforced this idea. Probation was also criticized. Many Americans thought criminals were getting off easy.

In response to the public outcry, the U.S. Congress and state lawmakers passed tough new sentencing laws. Determinate sentences, or sentences of fixed lengths, became the law. "Let the punishment fit the crime," became the slogan of the day. Crimes were placed into new categories based on the seriousness of the offense: the higher the category, the more serious the crime and the longer the sentence. The goal was to have each crime carry a fixed-length prison term. The term could not be reduced through good behavior. Inmates would be required to serve the entire sentence before they became eligible for parole

Many of the new sentencing laws were meant for repeat offenders, or "career criminals." Under the new laws, judges had less leeway in handing out prison terms. They could not look at an offender's background, history, and the particular circumstances of an offense. For example, a Michigan judge sentenced eighteen-year-old Gary Fannon to life in prison without the possibility of parole for possessing about 1.4 pounds (0.6 kilograms) of cocaine. The judge said:

> I have here a stack of letters from your family and friends. They are all glowing as to how good a person you are. The court believes all of these things. But this court has no discretion [freedom of decision making] whatsoever to give you any leniency. The legislators have determined the sentence in this case.

THREE-STRIKES LAWS

Politicians used the phrase "three strikes and you're out" to push tougher sentencing laws. The first three-strikes law was passed in the early 1990s in California. It came after a man on parole murdered a twelve-year-old girl. The man had two previous felonies. Supporters of the California law believed that repeat offenders like him should not be given the chance to commit further crimes. The law required judges to sentence offenders convicted of their third felony to twenty-five years to life in prison. Several other states passed similar laws. In 1994 the U.S. Congress passed a federal three-strikes law.

Three-strikes laws did not always produce the desired results. Nonviolent offenders were sometimes caught in its net. For example, in California a twenty-seven-year-old man with two prior robbery convictions was sentenced to twenty-five years to life in prison for stealing a slice of pepperoni pizza. Supporters of three-strikes laws argued that offenders were being fairly punished for a history of criminal activity. According to California deputy district attorney Bill Gravlin, "The people of California are sick of revolving-door justice, they're sick of judges who are soft on crime." Opponents of the three-strikes laws, on the other hand, found the laws excessive and harsh. According to Allan Parachini, spokesperson for the American Civil Liberties Union (ACLU, a national organization that works to preserve American constitutional rights), "No matter how many pizza thieves it sends to prison, this law is not going to make our streets safer."

Fixed-length sentencing gradually became more flexible. Lawmakers eased the strict guidelines. Judges were allowed a limited amount of discretion in deciding a convict's sentence. For example, a judge could look at a convict's prior record before issuing a sentence within a narrow sentence range.

PRISON POPULATION EXPLOSION

The use of crack cocaine in the United States increased drug use by the young and poor of U.S. inner cities. Easy and inexpensive to make, crack cocaine produces an immediate euphoria. This made it the drug of choice for many people. Under President Ronald Reagan, the U.S. government declared war on drugs. Congress passed tough new mandatory sentencing laws for drug-related offenses. Arrests for drug crimes skyrocketed. As a result, the prison population exploded. According to historian David Garland, "In the period from 1973 to 1997, the numbers of inmates incarcerated in the USA rose by more than 500 percent."

Prisons became severely overcrowded. At Stateville Penitentiary in Illinois, more than ten thousand prisoners shared cells that were built for four thousand. At a Maryland prison, an official stated, "If we emptied the prison today, we would be full tomorrow." The expanding prison population placed a huge burden on the entire criminal justice system. State and local governments rushed to build new facilities. Prison construction became big business. Construction could

Inmates at this state prison in California live in the gymnasium because of overcrowding.

not keep up with the growing demand, however. Overcrowding remained a huge problem.

Incarceration rates for African Americans rose at a faster rate than for white offenders. According to the Reverend Jesse Jackson, a prominent civil rights leader from Illinois, prison seemed like a step up for many of the nation's poorest residents. "Once they are jailed, they are no longer homeless," he said. "Once they are jailed, they have balanced meals." Jackson and others who studied poverty in the United States felt that life in the slums had grown so desperate that the threat of prison had lost its power to discourage people from breaking the law.

THE END OF REHABILITATION

Overcrowding in U.S. prisons led to many problems. Escapes, disease, and inmate-on-inmate violence increased in many prisons. Educational and recreational programs were cut back. Inmates faced long days of idleness. According to Stateville inmate Sam Gutierrez:

> It is the dull sameness of prison life, its idleness and boredom, that grinds me down. Nothing matters; everything is inconsequential [meaningless] other than when you will be free and how to make the time pass until then.

The tough-on-crime attitude across the nation meant that prisons no longer focused on rehabilitating inmates. The goal was to punish them for their mistakes. Long prison terms would remove criminals from society so they could do no further harm. Protecting the public became the central theme of penal policy in the United States.

BRINGING BACK WORK

The U.S. Congress lifted the ban on convict labor in 1979. Private employers began to hire inmates as a source of cheap labor. Inmates earned anywhere from twenty-five cents to seven dollars per hour. They worked at all kinds of jobs. Some worked at telemarketing or in the computer industry. Others raised hogs, packed golf balls, or made blue jeans. Prisoners also worked for the U.S. and state governments. Federal prisoners made uniforms, electronic equipment, and military helmets. State prisoners stamped license plates, painted school buses, and made prison furniture.

In 1995 Alabama became the first state to use chain-gang prison labor since the practice was abolished in the 1950s. Several other states have since adopted the practice. Southern chain gangs cut and trim plant growth along roadsides. They also break rocks and clean up litter. Northern chain gangs shovel snow after blizzards and clear public roads.

Those who support prisoner chain gangs think the sight of chained men on the side of a road acts as a public deterrent to crime. Public humiliation, they argue, will make people think twice about committing a

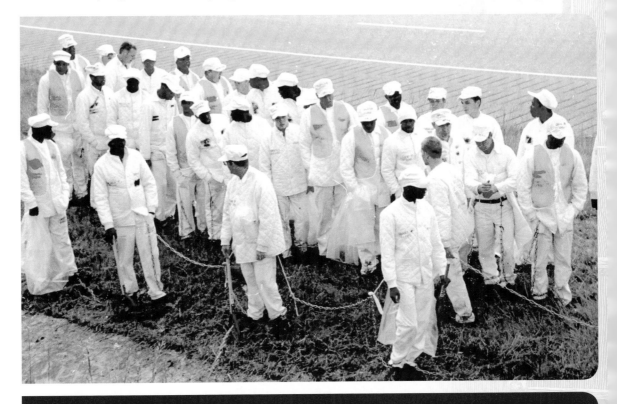

Prisoners from an Alabama correctional facility work on a chain gang in 1995.

crime. Alabama's prison commissioner Ron Jones said, "Every time a car passes and a child looks out on [the chain gang], they will reinforce the idea that crime has consequences." Those opposed to the practice think chain gangs violate human rights. Bud Meeks, executive director of the National Sheriff's Association, said, "Sitting in a cell is hard. It's hard on the mind, the body, the spirit. But a chain is degrading."

SUPERMAX PRISONS

The 1990s saw the growth of supermax prisons. These prisons are reserved for the most dangerous criminals. Inmates spend almost twenty-three hours each day confined to their cells. Guards monitor them with high-tech equipment, and human contact is minimal. Many politicians support supermax prisons because they want to be seen as tough on crime. The new prisons also bring jobs and money to communities that might otherwise face economic decline. But inmates in supermax prisons show an increase in mental illness. Many attempt suicide or suffer from hallucinations. Supermax prisons remain controversial. Human rights groups worry about the long-term effects on inmates. Many people believe mental health facilities should be built in their place.

PENALTIES FOR JUVENILE OFFENDERS

Crimes committed by juveniles increased in the early 1990s. Juvenile crime also became more severe. Criminal justice experts began to see an increase in murder among young criminals. Experts debated what the penalties should be for juvenile offenders. Some, such as Jeanine Pirro, district attorney for Westchester County, New York, wanted juveniles to face stricter penalties for their crimes. "For too long, we have been coddling young offenders," she said. "We have been reluctant to treat them as adults." Others, such as Judge Joseph West, disagreed. West believed young offenders should remain in the juvenile system. "The defendant may not have had the maturity to reason as an adult," he said, "and therefore he should not be punished as an adult."

Many states began to offer alternatives to prison for young offenders. Boot camps were designed to teach young lawbreakers respect for authority and self-discipline. To be eligible for boot camp, an offender had to be young, typically between eighteen and twenty-four years old. They had to be nonviolent first-time offenders or have a short history of minor offenses. Boot camp programs were modeled after military boot camps. Offenders lived at the camp between 90 and 180 days. The programs involved physical and mental discipline and military drills. They also included education, job training, and drug abuse treatment. Many juvenile boot camp programs had after-care services to help young offenders return to school and find jobs.

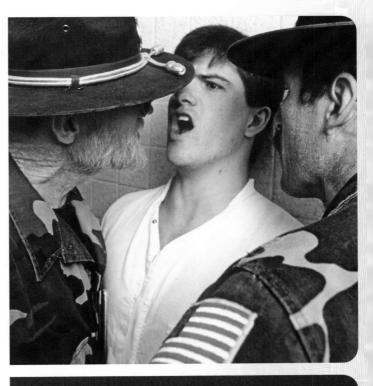

A juvenile offender *(center)* experiences the first day at a Montana prison boot camp.

THE RETURN OF THE DEATH PENALTY

By the late 1970s, most Americans supported the death penalty. They considered it a just punishment for murder and other serious crimes. Professor Ernest van den Haag of Fordham University in New York City expressed the thoughts of many when he said, "I think justice requires that those who take someone else's life do not survive the victim." Many people also believed the death penalty discouraged people from committing crimes.

In 1976, in the case of *Gregg v. Georgia*, the U.S. Supreme Court ruled that the death penalty was constitutional. The Court examined Troy

Gregg's trial for two counts of murder and found that the state of Georgia had protected his constitutional rights. They found no evidence of prejudice or wrongdoing in his sentencing. The Court's decision opened the door for executions to begin again. On January 17, 1977, Gary Gilmore was the first person to be executed in the United States since 1968. Found guilty of murdering two people, Gilmore was shot by a firing squad in Utah. Within the next few years, more than thirty states were using capital punishment again. The majority of executions take place in the South, sometimes called the death belt by criminal justice experts. The State of Texas executes the most prisoners.

In 1982 the State of Texas began executing convicts by injecting them with needles full of chemicals that kill them. It quickly became the most common method of execution in the United States. Two death row inmates in Kentucky challenged the use of lethal injection. They claimed it caused unnecessary pain and suffering. In 2006 the Supreme Court upheld the use of lethal injection. The Court ruled in *Baze v. Rees* that lethal injection does not violate the Eighth Amendment ban on cruel and unusual punishment.

The debate over capital punishment continues. Fourteen states have replaced the death penalty with life in prison without the possibility of parole. The number of executions has declined in recent years. Several Supreme Court rulings have limited the number of convicts that can be executed. In 2003 the Court banned executions for the mentally ill. In 2005 the court banned the death penalty for offenders who committed their crime as juveniles. And in 2008, the Court ruled that the death penalty can only be used for the crime of murder.

Public opinion has shifted. Many people are currently working to abolish the death penalty. They cite the fact that the United States is the only industrialized Western nation that executes convicts. Many criminal justice experts believe that the death penalty does not deter murderers. Others object on the grounds that the death penalty is not applied fairly to all people convicted of similar crimes. Those in favor of capital punishment believe that executing people who commit murder is simply justice. Their arguments focus on the victims of crime rather than the criminal. The question of capital punishment in the United States is far from settled. With more than three thousand inmates on death row in 2008, it remains a prominent issue.

THE PRISON REVOLVING DOOR

Tougher sentences, longer prison terms, and the death penalty have not eliminated crime in the United States. Released prisoners continue to commit new crimes. According to U.S. Bureau of Justice statistics, 60 to 70 percent of inmates return to a life of crime after their release from prison. Rearrests are highest in the first year. In his book, *Behind the Walls*, journalist and prison inmate Jorge Antonio Renaud explained why so many convicts return to crime:

> If you lock up a man for years on end, deny him a chance to use his skills or learn new ones, impress upon him that he is basically a life-long loser, then release him back into society without social skills, coping skills, relationship skills, and with fifty dollars in his pocket: you are sorely mistaken if you believe that man, especially if he has no family to help, will be able to stay afloat and find a place in society.

The history of the U.S. penal system is not a happy story. But in the twenty-first century, there are programs that are working to close the prison revolving door and restore former inmates to productive lives in society.

Society is not going to adjust to us.
We have to adjust to society.

—ALBERTO LOPEZ, NEW YORK STATE PRISON INMATE, 2008

CHAPTER NINE

WHAT'S NEXT?

The United States was founded on the principles of freedom and liberty for all citizens. Yet the United States locks up a higher percentage of its population than any other nation. In the twenty-first century, more than two million people are serving terms in prisons and jails in the United States. Men are more likely than women to go to prison. African American men are more likely to serve time than Latino or white men.

The United States spends more than forty billion dollars each year on incarceration. Taxpayers shoulder this huge cost. When money is scarce and budgets need to be cut, funds for education, health care, and social welfare programs often suffer. Some states spend more on prisons than on higher education. Many criminal justice experts believe the billions of prison dollars would be better spent on programs to keep people out of prison. Better education, housing, and social service programs, they argue, would eliminate the factors that lead to crime. With less crime, there would be less need for prisons.

In addition to the monetary costs, imprisonment also imposes high human costs. According to the wife of a former inmate:

> Those who get in trouble all the time think it only affects them, but they are wrong. It affects the whole family, mother, father, sister and brother. The family, as well as the offender, has to live with the consequences. The shame and guilt are carried for many years.

Jobs are scarce for former inmates. Families are damaged. Children of inmates often suffer from emotional and behavioral problems. More than 1.5 million U.S. children have at least one parent in prison or jail. Studies have found that children of prison inmates often face high-risk futures.

A girl talks with her mother through glass during a prison visit.

GET OUT AND STAY OUT!

Despite a long history of legal punishment—from the whipping post to rehabilitation to locking up offenders and throwing away the key—crime is still a serious problem in the United States. Spending on prisons continues to grow. But studies show that the increase in incarceration has not reduced crime. Few offenders change for the better in prison. In fact, the longer a person is in prison, the less likely that person will be a productive citizen when released.

Most inmates are eventually released from prison. More than two-thirds of them will be rearrested for a new offense within three years of their release. According to JoAnne Page, executive director of an ex-offender self-help group, "The culture of violence, whether it is reinforced or learned for the first time in jail and prison, leaves the institution walls in the souls and the internal scar tissue of prisoners upon their release, and is brought home with them to their families and communities."

Prison is but one solution to the problem of crime. According to attorney Russell Burdett, "Locking somebody up in jail is an easy thing to do. It doesn't take a whole lot of effort. You walk him to a cell. You open a door. You push him in it, and you close the door. That's the easy way out." Criminologists (scientists who study criminal behavior) are searching for more effective ways for offenders to pay their debt to society and be restored to lives as productive citizens.

A prisoner on house arrest shows his electronic leg bracelet.

ALTERNATIVES TO PRISON

Prisons of the twenty-first century are overcrowded and expensive to run. For this reason, some judges are imposing intermediate sanctions. These sentences are designed to punish offenders without sending them to prison. For example, probation with intensive supervision means that the offender must report frequently to a probation officer. Offenders are watched twenty-four hours a day. They must wear electronic bands on their wrists or ankles to monitor their whereabouts. Offenders must be employed full-time. In many cases, they must attend counseling classes. Offenders convicted of drug-related crimes must participate in drug-treatment programs. They must also undergo periodic blood and urine testing for drug use.

Some intermediate sanctions require offenders to work and use a portion of their earnings to pay back their victim. For property crimes, they must repay the value of the amount stolen. If the victim was physically injured, offenders must pay their medical bills. Judges look at the seriousness of the offense, the impact on the victim, and the offender's ability to pay when they issue these types of sanctions.

Some offenders are sentenced to probation with the condition that they perform community service. They work in the community without pay for a certain number of hours, usually six hours of work in place of one day in jail. The idea behind this sentencing is that the offender hurt the community in some way. He or she must pay back the community with some form of labor. Offenders work for neighborhood groups. They paint low-income housing units, clear litter from playgrounds, and sweep around public buildings.

THE RETURN OF SHAMING

Some judges have returned to the colonial sentence of shaming to punish people convicted of crimes. In Texas, Judge Ted Poe sentenced more than three hundred offenders to "public notice" sentences. In one instance, a man who beat his wife was ordered to apologize to her on the steps of city hall. In another case, Judge Poe ordered a man convicted of accidental homicide to parade in front of a bar with a sign that read, "I killed two people while driving drunk." According to Poe, "Most of us care about what people think of us. If we are held up to public ridicule, we don't like it and two things will happen. We will change our conduct and our attitudes."

Another program that is gaining popularity is the Victim-Offender Mediation Program (VOMP). The focus of the program is on victims of crime. Offenders meet face-to-face with the victims of their crimes and a trained mediator. Victims tell their offenders how the crime affected them, ask questions, and share their feelings. Offenders see the pain their actions caused and take responsibility for their crimes. They may offer an explanation or apologize. The victim and offender work out an agreement that is meaningful to both of them to restore the victims' losses in some way. The agreement can be a monetary settlement or some other way for the offender to make amends. Sometimes the offender works for the victim or does community service.

Most victim-offender mediations work with juvenile offenders who committed nonviolent crimes. The goal is to keep young offenders out of prison. For violent crimes, such as rape or murder, the victim or the victim's family can request mediation. It does not replace incarceration. The offender still goes to prison. But mediation allows healing and closure for the victim or the victim's family. Most victims report that meeting with the offender helps them move forward with their lives after the crime. And after facing their victims, offenders commit fewer and less serious crimes than similar offenders who did not participate in the program.

Although alternative sanctions are becoming more common, thousands of offenders are still sentenced to prison each year. When they have served their time, most inmates find the transition from prison to the outside world extremely difficult. Many have no family to return to or to support them. They face social stigma and often find it difficult to get a job. "The businessman, if you ask him to hire a one-time offender, to give an ex-con a chance, refuses to have anything to do with him," said Professor Henry Ruth Jr. of the University of Pennsylvania Law School. "I don't see how you can scream about crime and then say, 'I won't hire any man who has been in prison.' If a first-offender comes out of prison and can't get a job, he has only one alternative: to go back to crime. He has to live."

PROGRAMS THAT WORK

Prison ministries such as Economic Opportunities (EcOp) in Memphis, Tennessee, help released inmates successfully transition to life outside of prison. This faith-based program works with the U.S. government and the Tennessee Board of Probation and Parole. EcOp helps former inmates find steady jobs. Many ex-convicts cannot find jobs because of their criminal history. According to Jim Kennedy, the director of EcOp, "One felony conviction reduces a person's earning potential by 40 percent." Economic Opportunities works to change that bleak statistic.

EcOp partners with for-profit businesses. It provides jobs, personal attention, and intensive support to former inmates. Most participants in the program lack formal education. They have limited job skills. EcOp helps them find full-time jobs and holds them accountable for their behavior and

An inmate *(left)* talks to an outreach representative *(right)* at a transition fair at a correctional facility in Minnesota. Reformers continue to search for programs that will keep former convicts out of prison.

work. The participants acknowledge past mistakes and accept responsibility for their actions. They also learn strategies to change their behavior.

Former inmates take part in the EcOp program for six to twelve months. They attend daily Bible studies after work. Former addicts undergo random drug tests. Those who need it are given help earning their GED (equivalent to a high school diploma). They may also receive help obtaining a driver's license. Former inmates learn how to manage their money and balance a checkbook. Graduates of the program have great success. According to Thomas F. Norman at Barnhart Crane & Rigging Company, "I have hired three solid men from the program and they are truly doing a superb job. . . . We need to continue to provide the opportunity and support for these young men to succeed and become solid citizens of the community."

I Can't We Can (ICWC) is a drug-abuse recovery program. It helps many former prisoners in Baltimore, Maryland. Israel Cason founded the program. Cason is a recovered addict who spent time in jail for drug-related offenses. He has faith in the value of addicts helping addicts. Cason believes in a holistic approach to recovery. He considers each aspect of an addict's life in relation to his or her recovery. Cason quotes the ancient Greek philosopher Plato when he reminds participants, "The parts can never be well unless the whole is well." ICWC combines spiritual elements, tough love, job training, health care, and drug treatment. The program also includes education. It offers GED classes and parenting classes.

Participants in the program live in residential housing units for one year. The program receives charitable contributions and community support. I Can't We Can has opened a thrift store, a barbershop, a moving company, a construction company, a dollar store, and a supermarket to fund its efforts. Seventy-five percent of the former addicts who have completed the program have stayed out of prison. Some return to school and obtain college degrees. Others work within the organization or find steady jobs in the community. They receive encouragement and support through an ICWC alumni association.

WHAT'S NEXT?

Crime and punishment are woven into the fabric of our nation's history. In every era, some Americans have wanted to turn convicts into useful citizens. Others have wanted only to punish them. The high recidivism rate proves that the current correctional strategies are not working. Experts agree that the majority of prison inmates are more violent and less connected to their communities when they leave prison than when they entered.

As Americans move forward into the twenty-first century, we, as citizens of a democracy, must find answers to some tough questions. How do we keep citizens safe? What type of punishment should criminals face when they break the law? What obligations do we have to the victims of crime? Do those obligations outweigh the constitutional charge to treat prisoners humanely? Should we continue to build prisons, or should we increase the use of intermediate sanctions, probation, and parole? Should prisons be responsible for educating, rehabilitating, and training inmates? What are the best methods to accomplish these goals? Is the death penalty a violation of a prisoner's civil rights?

The way we answer these questions will determine the future of the U.S. penal system. Communities must work together to find the answers. No one person, one program, or one plan will solve the complex problems of crime and punishment. According to former prisoner and recovered heroin addict Israel Cason, "I can not. We can!"

U.S. prison inmates have created thousands of poems, songs, and books about their experiences behind bars. Malcolm Braly, a native of Portland, Oregon, became an author while in prison. Abandoned by his parents, Braly spent his childhood alternating between foster homes and institutions for delinquent children. He spent nearly seventeen years in California's San Quentin Prison, Nevada State Prison, and Folsom State Prison for various burglary convictions. Braly wrote three novels behind bars. After he was released from prison in 1965, he wrote *On the Yard, False Starts: A Memoir of San Quentin and Other Prisons*, and *The Protector*. His books received critical acclaim. Malcolm Braly enjoyed fifteen years of freedom before he died in a car accident at the age of fifty-four. The following excerpt is from *False Starts*, which describes his experience with incarceration.

The hardest part of serving time is the predictability. Each day moves like every other. You *know* nothing different can happen. You focus on tiny events, a movie scheduled weeks ahead, your reclass [reclassification by the prison staff], your parole hearing, things far in the future, and slowly, smooth day by day, draw them to you. There will be no glad surprise, no spontaneous holiday, and a month from now, six months, a year, you will be just where you are, doing just what you're doing, except you'll be older.

This airless calm is produced by rigid routine. Custody doesn't encourage spontaneity. Walk slow, the Cynic says, and don't make any fast moves. Each morning you know where evening will find you. There is no way to avoid your cell. When everyone marched into the block you would be left alone in

the empty yard. Each Monday describes every Friday. Holidays in prison are only another mark of passing time and for many they are the most difficult days. Most of the outrages that provide such lurid passages in the folklore of our prisons are inspired by boredom. Some grow so weary of this grinding sameness they will drink wood alcohol even though they are aware this potent toxin may blind or kill them. Others fight with knives to the death and the survivor will remark, "It was just something to do."

The interior of San Quentin in the 1950s

1718: Transportation of more than thirty thousand British convicts to the American colonies begins.

1764: Cesare Beccaria's essay *On Crimes and Punishment* is published.

1775: Transportation of British convicts to the American colonies ends.

1790: Philadelphia's Walnut Street Jail, the first penitentiary in the United States, opens.

1821: New York's Auburn Prison opens with the silent system of prison discipline.

1829: Philadelphia's Eastern State Penitentiary opens with the separate system of prison discipline.

1861: The Civil War begins.

1865: The Civil War ends.

1870: The National Prison Congress adopts its Declaration of Principles.

1873: The first prison completely devoted to women, the Indiana Reformatory Institution for Women and Girls, opens.

1876: The Elmira reformatory opens in Elmira, New York.

1899: The Illinois legislature passes the Juvenile Court Act and establishes the first juvenile court in the United States.

1908: The American Prison Association is created. The Federal Bureau of Investigation (FBI) is created.

1910: Congress passes the Mann Act to fight prostitution across state lines.

1914: Congress passes the Harrison Narcotic Act to make it illegal to sell drugs without a prescription from a medical doctor.

1920: Prohibition goes into effect. Prison investigator Frank Tannenbaum tours U.S. prisons and investigates prison conditions.

1929: The stock market crashes, and the Great Depression begins.

1930: The Federal Bureau of Prisons is created.

1931: *The Report on Penal Institutions, Probation, and Parole* is published, detailing the miserable condition of U.S. prisons. Attica Prison opens in Attica, New York.

1932: Congress passes the Lindbergh Law to make kidnapping a federal crime.

1933: Prohibition ends.

1934: Alcatraz prison, on an island off San Francisco, California, becomes a federal prison.

1941: The United States enters World War II.

1945: World War II ends.

1950: The FBI begins the "Ten Most Wanted" program.

1954: The American Prison Association changes its name to the American Correctional Association.

1955: The United Nations publishes the *Standard Minimum Rules for the Treatment of Prisoners*.

1957: The FBI begins its Top Hoodlum program.

1961: The United States sends its first U.S. troops to Vietnam.

1963: President John F. Kennedy is assassinated.

1965: President Lyndon Johnson creates the President's Crime Commission.

1966: The *Miranda* decision requires police officers to inform people arrested for crimes that they are allowed to have an attorney present during questioning.

1968: Dr. Martin Luther King Jr. is assassinated. Robert F. Kennedy is assassinated.

1971: The Stanford Prison Experiment proves that prisons change the behavior of inmates and guards. The Attica Prison riot sheds light on the problems in most U.S. prisons.

1972: Capital punishment is abolished in the United States.

1974: *The Martinson Report* on the failures of correctional treatment is published.

1975: The Vietnam War ends.

1976: Capital punishment is declared constitutional by the U.S. Supreme Court.

1982: Lethal injection is used for the first time for legal executions in Texas.

1991: Economic Opportunities—a faith-based program for released prisoners that helps them find jobs and transition to life outside of prison—is created in Memphis, Tennessee.

1995: Alabama reintroduces chain gangs.

1997: I Can't We Can, Inc., is created in Baltimore, Maryland, to help drug addicts and former inmates become drug free and self-sufficient.

2003: The U.S. Supreme Court rules that executing intellectually challenged offenders is cruel and unusual punishment and violates the Eighth Amendment of the Constitution.

2005: The U.S. Supreme Court bans executions of offenders who were under the age of eighteen years old when they committed their crimes.

2006: The U.S. Supreme Court upholds the use of lethal injections for executions.

2008: The U.S. Supreme Court rules that capital punishment can only be used in murder cases.

SOURCE NOTES

6   Carl Bridenbaugh, *Cities in Revolt: Urban Life in America, 1743–1776* (New York: Alfred A. Knopf, 1955), 301.

7   A. Roger Ekirch, *Bound for America: The Transportation of British Convicts to the Colonies, 1718–1775* (New York: Oxford University Press, 1987), 23.

7   Ibid., 139.

8   John C. Miller, *The First Frontier: Life in Colonial America* (Lanham, MD: University Press of America, 1986), 87.

9   Lawrence M. Friedman, *Crime and Punishment in American History* (New York: HarperCollins BasicBooks, 1993), 42.

10   Louis B. Wright and Marion Tinling, eds., *The Secret Diary of William Byrd of Westover, 1709–1712* (Richmond: Dietz Press, 1941), 585.

11   Blake McKelvey, *American Prisons: A History of Good Intentions* (Montclair, NJ: Patterson Smith, 1977), 3.

12   S. G. Howe, *Report of a Minority of the Special Committee of the Boston Prison Discipline Society, May 27, 1845* (Boston: William D. Ticknor and Company, 1846), 15–16.

12–13 Bridenbaugh, 118.

13   Cesare Beccaria, *On Crimes and Punishments: Of the Punishment of Death*, 1764, reprint, *Crimetheory.com*, January 23, 2002, http://www.crimetheory.com/Archive/Beccaria/Beccaria00a.htm (May 29, 2007).

15   J. P. Brissot de Warville, *New Travels in the United States Of America, 1788*, ed. Durand Echeverria, trans. Mara Soceanu Vamos and Durand Echeverria (1788; repr., Cambridge, Mass: The Belknap Press of Harvard University Press, 1992), 296.

16   Benjamin Rush, "An Enquiry into the Effects of Public Punishments upon Criminals, and upon Society," in *Essays: Literary, Moral and Philosophical* (Schenectady, NY: Union College Press, 1988), 80.

16   Ibid., 89.

19–20 Orlando F. Lewis, *The Development of American Prisons and Prison Customs, 1776–1845* (1922; repr., Montclair, NJ: Patterson, 1967), 81.

20   Alexis de Tocqueville and Gustave de Beaumont, *On the Penitentiary*

95

System in the United States and Its Application in France (1833; repr., Carbondale: Southern Illinois University Press, 1964), 163.

20–11 Torsten Eriksson, *The Reformers: An Historical Survey of Pioneer Experiments in the Treatment of Criminals* (New York: Elsevier Scientific, 1976), 62–63.

21–22 David J. Rothman, *The Discovery of the Asylum: Social Order and Disorder in the New Republic* (Boston: Little, Brown and Company, 1971), 85.

22 Charles Dickens, *American Notes and Pictures from Italy* (1842; repr., London: Oxford University Press, 1957), 100–101.

23 Mary Carpenter, *Our Convicts* (1864; repr., Montclair, NJ: Patterson Smith, 1969), 2:207.

24 Enoch Cobb Wines, ed., *Transactions of the National Congress on Penitentiary and Reformatory Discipline, Held at Cincinnati, Ohio, October 12–18, 1870* (Albany, NY: Argus Company, Printers, 1871), 541.

25 Patrick C. Murphy, *Behind Gray Walls* (Caldwell, ID: Caxton Printers, 1927), 41–42.

26 Leon F. Litwack, *Been in the Storm So Long: The Aftermath of Slavery* (New York: Vintage Books, 1980), 284.

27 Wines, 38.

28 Zebulon Reed Brockway, *The Ideal of a True Prison System for a State* (1869; repr., *Crimetheory.com*, January 23, 2002, http://www.crimetheory.com/Archive/Zeb1/ZebPrint.htm (May 25, 2007), 20.

29 Murphy, 23.

30 Brockway, *The Ideal of a True Prison System for a State*, 35–36.

30 Zebulon Reed Brockway, "The American Reformatory Prison System," *American Journal of Sociology,* January 1910, 477.

32 Harry Elmer Barnes, *The Story of Punishment: A Record of Man's Inhumanity to Man*, 2nd ed, rev. (Montclair, NJ: Patterson Smith, 1972), 181.

34 Frank Tannenbaum, *Wall Shadows: A Study in American Prisons* (New York: G. P. Putnam's Sons, 1922), ix.

35 Friedman, 335.

35 Kevin B. O'Reilly, "Confronting Eugenics: Does the New Discredited Practice Have Relevance to Today's Technology?" *American Medical Association News* (*amednews.com*), July 3, 2007, http://biopoliticaltimes .org/article.php?id=3503&&printsafe=1 (September 3, 2007).

37 David J. Rothman, *Conscience and Convenience* (Boston: Little, Brown and Company, 1980), 89.

38 Isidore Zimmerman, *Punishment Without Crime* (New York: Clarkson N. Potter, 1964), 174.

38 Kate Richards O'Hare, *In Prison* (1923; repr., Seattle: University of Washington Press, 1976), 65.

39 Tannenbaum, 107.

39 Ibid., 141.

39 Ibid., ix.

39 Thomas Mott Osborne, *Within Prison Walls: Being a Narrative of Personal Experience during a Week of Voluntary Confinement in the State Prison at Auburn, New York* (1914; repr., Montclair, NJ: Patterson Smith, 1969), 323.

39–40 Thomas Mott Osborne, *Society and Prisons* (New Haven, CT: Yale University Press, 1916), 154.

40 Ibid., 163–164.

41 Frank Tannenbaum, *Osborne of Sing Sing* (Chapel Hill: University of North Carolina Press, 1933), 179–180.

42 Victor F. Nelson, *Prison Days and Nights* (Boston: Little, Brown, and Company, 1934), 150.

42–43 Frank Richard Prassel, *The Great American Outlaw: A Legacy of Fact and Fiction* (Norman: University of Oklahoma Press, 1993), 271.

43 H. Bruce Franklin, *The Victim as Criminal and Artist: Literature from the American Prison* (New York: Oxford University Press, 1978), 169.

44–45 George W. Wickersham, *The Report on Penal Institutions, Probation and Parole* (Washington DC: U.S. Government Printing Office, 1931), 170.

46–47 David A. Ward, "Alcatraz and Marion: Confinement in Super Maximum Custody," in *Escaping Prison Myths: Selected Topics in the History of Federal Corrections* (Washington DC: American University Press, 1994), 83.

47 Ibid., 87.

48 John Bartlow Martin, *Break Down the Walls* (New York: Ballantine Books, 1954), 122.

48 Bill Sands, *My Shadow Ran Fast* (Englewood Cliffs, NJ: Prentice-Hall, 1964), 54.

48–49 Wilbur G. Lewis, "Attica Prison to Be Convicts' Paradise," *New York Times*, August 2, 1931.

49 Zimmerman, 152.

50 *New York Times*, "Negro Burglar Gets Life in Alabama for $1.50 Theft," October 1, 1936.

51 United Nations, "Standard Minimum Rules for the Treatment of Prisoners," adopted by the First United Nations Congress on the Prevention of Crime and the Treatment of Offenders, Geneva, 1955, 9

53 Gladys A. Erickson, "Medicine in Prison," *Warden Ragen of Joliet* (New York: E. P. Dutton & Company, 1985), 206–207.

54 James V. Bennett, *Federal Prisons, 1948* (Leavenworth, KS: United States Penitentiary, 1949), 3.

55 Malcolm Braly, *False Starts: A Memoir of San Quentin and Other Prisons* (Boston: Little, Brown and Company, 1976), 157–158.

57 United Nations, 10.

58 Randall Kennedy, *Race, Crime, and the Law* (New York: Vintage Books, 1998), 62.

59 Alex Haley, *The Autobiography of Malcolm X: As Told to Alex Haley* (New York: Ballantine Books, 1964), 272.

60 Eldridge Cleaver, *Soul on Ice* (New York: Dell Publishing, 1968), 81.

61 Jerome Washington, *Iron House: Stories from the Yard* (New York: Vintage Books, 1995), 17.

62 Fred J. Cook, "There's Always a Crime Wave—How Bad Is This One?" *New York Times*, October 6, 1968.

63 American Bar Association, "The Miranda Rule," *Family Legal Guide*, 2002, http://criminal.findlaw.com/articles/1443.html (November 9, 2007).

64   Fred P. Graham, *The Self-Inflicted Wound* (New York: Macmillan, 1970), 14.

64   Ibid., 109.

65   Malcolm M. Feeley and Austin D. Sarat, *The Policy Dilemma: Federal Crime Policy and the Law Enforcement Assistance Administration* (Minneapolis: University of Minnesota Press, 1980), 37.

65   James Vorenberg, "The President's Commission on Law Enforcement and Administration of Justice," *Criminology*, vol. 4, May 1966, 57.

65–66   Jack Henry Abbott, *In the Belly of the Beast: Letters from Prison* (New York: Vintage Books, 1991), 14.

66   *Death Row in Our Town*, DVD, produced and directed by Ali Pomeroy (New York: Lumiere Productions and Tapestry International, 2000).

67   Cook.

68   Bert Useem and Peter Kimball, *States of Siege: U.S. Prison Riots, 1971–1986* (New York: Oxford University Press, 1991), 236.

70   Dave Grusin and M. Ames, "Keep Your Eye on the Sparrow," (New York: Universal Music Group, 1975).

72   Mike Sager, "The Case of Gary Fannon," *Rolling Stone*, September 3, 1992.

72   Eric Slater, "Pizza Thief Gets 25 Years to Life," *Los Angeles Times*, March 3, 1995.

72   Ibid.

73   David Garland, *The Culture of Control: Crime and Social Order in Contemporary Society* (Chicago: University of Chicago Press, 2001), 14.

73   *U.S. News & World Report*, "Crisis in the Prisons: Not Enough Room for All the Criminals," November 28, 1977, 77.

74   Don Terry, "Prison As Usual: A Special Report," *New York Times*, September 13, 1992.

74   Norval Morris, "The Contemporary Prison: 1965–Present," in Norval Morris and David J. Rothman, eds., *The Oxford History of the Prison: The Practice of Punishment in Western Society* (New York: Oxford University Press, 1998), 203.

76   Rick Bragg, "Chain Gangs to Return to Roads of Alabama," *New York Times*, March 26, 1995.

76   Ibid.

76   Elsa Brenner, "New Debate on Penalties for Juvenile Offenders," *New York Times*, February 18, 1996.

76   Ibid.

77   *Crime File: The Death Penalty*, James Wilson, moderator, VHS (Rockville, MD: National Institute of Justice, 1985).

79   Jorge Antonio Renaud, *Behind the Walls: A Guide for Family and Friends of Texas Inmates* (Denton: University of North Texas Press, 2002), 57–58.

80   Hubert B. Herring, "For Ex-Inmates, Getting a Job Is the First Step to Stability," *New York Times*, January 29, 2006.

81   Catrina Williams, "Michael Is No Longer Dirty," *Economic Opportunities Newsletter*, May 2007, 2.

82   JoAnne Page, "Violence and Incarceration: A Personal Observation," in John P. May and Khalid R. Pitts, eds., *Building Violence: How America's Rush to Incarcerate Creates More Violence* (Thousand Oaks, CA: Sage Publications, Inc., 2000), 138.

82   *Burden of Justice: Alternatives to Prison Overcrowding*, produced, directed, and edited David Ellis, VHS (Toluca Lake, CA: Ellis Productions, 1991).

83   Dean E. Murphy, "The Nation; Justice as a Morality Play That Ends with Shame," *New York Times*, June 3, 2001.

83   Ibid.

84   Cook.

85   Jim Kennedy, director of *Economic Opportunities*, telephone conversation with author, November 27, 2007.

86   Thomas F. Norman, director of maintenance at Barnhart Crane & Rigging Company, letter to Jim Kennedy, *Economic Opportunities*, July 19, 2007.

86   John L. Mica, *Alternatives to Incarceration: What Works and Why?* House of Representatives Subcommittee on Criminal Justice, Drug Policy, and Human Resources (Washington DC: U. S. Government Printing Office, 2001), 149.

87   Israel Cason, "CEO's Corner," 2006, *I Can't We Can*. http://icantwecan/org/ceocorner.html (January 1, 2008).

Abbott, Jack Henry. *In the Belly of the Beast: Letters from Prison*. New York: Vintage Books, 1991.

Barnes, Harry Elmer. *The Story of Punishment: A Record of Man's Inhumanity to Man*. 2nd ed., rev. Montclair, NJ: Patterson Smith, 1972.

Beccaria, Cesare. *On Crimes and Punishments*. 1764. Reprint. Indianapolis, IN: The Bobbs-Merrill Company, 1963.

Braly, Malcolm. *False Starts: A Memoir of San Quentin and Other Prisons*. Boston: Little, Brown and Company, 1976.

Bridenbaugh, Carl. *Cities In Revolt: Urban Life in America, 1743–1776*. New York: Alfred A. Knopf, 1955.

Brissot de Warville, J. P. *New Travels In the United States Of America: 1788*. 1791. Reprint. Cambridge, MA: The Belknap Press of Harvard University Press, 1964.

Carpenter, Mary. *Our Convicts*. Vols. 1 and 2. 1864. Reprint, Montclair, NJ: Patterson Smith, 1969.

Christianson, Scott. *With Liberty for Some: 500 Years of Imprisonment in America*. Boston: Northeastern University Press, 1998.

Ekirch, A. Roger. *Bound For America: The Transportation of British Convicts to the Colonies 1718–1775*. New York: Oxford University Press, 1987.

Erickson, Gladys A. *Warden Ragen of Joliet*. New York: E. P. Dutton & Company, 1957.

Eriksson, Torsten. *The Reformers: An Historical Survey of Pioneer Experiments in the Treatment of Criminals*. New York: Elsevier Scientific, 1976.

Feeley, Malcolm M. and Austin D. Sarat. *The Policy Dilemma: Federal Crime Policy and the Law Enforcement Assistance Administration*. Minneapolis: University of Minnesota Press, 1980.

Franklin, H. Bruce. *The Victim as Criminal and Artist: Literature from the American Prison*. New York: Oxford University Press, 1978.

Freedman, Estelle B. *Their Sisters' Keepers: Women's Prison Reform in America, 1830–1930*. Ann Arbor: University of Michigan Press, 1984.

Friedman, Lawrence M. *Crime and Punishment in American History*. New York: HarperCollins BasicBooks, 1993.

Garland, David. *The Culture of Control: Crime and Social Order in Contemporary Society*. Chicago: University of Chicago Press, 2001.

Graham, Fred P. *The Self-Inflicted Wound*. New York: Macmillan, 1970.

Herman, Peter G., editor. *The American Prison System*. New York: H. W. Wilson Company, 2001.

Hirsch, Adam Jay. *The Rise of the Penitentiary: Prisons and Punishment in Early America*. New Haven, CT: Yale University Press, 1992.

Ignatieff, Michael. *A Just Measure of Pain: The Penitentiary in the Industrial Revolution, 1750–1850*. New York: Pantheon Books, 1978.

Jacobs, James B. *Stateville: The Penitentiary in Mass Society*. Chicago: University of Chicago Press, 1977.

Kennedy, Randall. *Race, Crime, and the Law*. New York: Vintage Books, 1998.

Lewis, Orlando F. *The Development of American Prisons and Prison Customs, 1776–1845*. 1922. Reprint, Montclair, NJ: Patterson Smith, 1967.

Lyons, Lewis. *The History of Punishment*. London: Amber Books, 2003.

Martin, John Bartlow. *Break Down the Walls*. New York: Ballantine Books, 1954.

May, John P., ed. *Building Violence: How America's Rush to Incarcerate Creates More Violence*. Thousand Oaks, CA: Sage Publications, 2000.

McKelvey, Blake. *American Prisons: A History of Good Intentions*. Montclair, NJ: Patterson Smith, 1977.

Morris, Norval. *The Future of Imprisonment*. Chicago: University of Chicago Press, 1974.

Morris, Norval, and David J. Rothman, eds. *The Oxford History of the Prison: The Practice of Punishment in Western Society*. New York: Oxford University Press, 1998.

Murphy, Patrick C. *Behind Gray Walls*. Caldwell, ID: Caxton Printers, 1927.

Nelson, Victor F. *Prison Days and Nights*. Boston: Little, Brown, and Company, 1934.

Oakey, Mary Hostetler. *Journey from the Gallows Historical: Evolution of the Penal Philosophies and Practices in the Nation's Capital*. Lanham, MD: University Press of America, 1988.

O'Hare, Kate Richards. *In Prison*. 1923. Reprint, Seattle: University of Washington Press, 1976.

Osborne, Thomas Mott. *Society and Prisons*. New Haven, CT: Yale University Press, 1916.

————. *Within Prison Walls: Being a Narrative of Personal Experience during a Week of Voluntary Confinement in the State Prison at Auburn, New York*. 1914. Reprint, Montclair, NJ: Patterson Smith, 1969.

Rafter, Nicole Hahn. *Partial Justice: Women, Prisons, and Social Control*. New Brunswick, NJ: Transaction Publishers, 1990.

Renaud, Jorge Antonio. *Behind the Walls: A Guide for Family and Friends of Texas Inmates*. Denton: University of North Texas Press, 2002.

Roberts, John W., ed. *Escaping Prison Myths: Selected Topics in the History of Federal Corrections*. Washington, DC: American University Press, 1994.

Ross, Jeffrey Ian and Stephen C. Richards. *Behind Bars: Surviving Prison.* Indianapolis, IN: Alpha Books, 2002.

Roth, Mitchel P. *Crime and Punishment: A History of the Criminal Justice System.* Belmont, CA: Thomson Wadsworth, 2005.

Rothman, David J. *Conscience and Convenience.* Boston: Little, Brown and Company, 1980.

———. *The Discovery of the Asylum: Social Order and Disorder in the New Republic.* Boston: Little, Brown and Company, 1971.

Sands, Bill. *My Shadow Ran Fast.* Englewood Cliffs, NJ: Prentice-Hall, 1964.

Sullivan, Larry E., editor. *Bandits & Bibles: Convict Literature in Nineteenth-Century America.* New York: Akashic Books, 2003.

———. *The Prison Reform Movement: Forlorn Hope.* Boston: Twayne Publishers, 1990.

Sykes, Gresham. *The Society of Captives: A Study of a Maximum Security Prison.* 1958. Reprint. Princeton, NJ: Princeton University Press, 2007.

Tannenbaum, Frank. *Osborne of Sing Sing.* Chapel Hill: University of North Carolina Press, 1933.

———. *Wall Shadows: A Study in American Prisons.* New York: G. P. Putnam's Sons, 1922.

Teeters, Negley K. *The Cradle of the Penitentiary: The Walnut Street Jail at Philadelphia, 1773–1835.* Philadelphia: Pennsylvania Prison Society, 1955.

Tonry, Michael, ed. *The Future of Imprisonment.* New York: Oxford University Press, 2004.

Walker, Samuel. *Popular Justice: A History of American Criminal Justice.* New York: Oxford University Press, 1998.

Bayer, Linda N., and Austin Sarat. *Drugs, Crime, and Criminal Justice.* Philadelphia: Chelsea House, 2001.

Benson, Michael. *Malcolm X.* Minneapolis: Twenty-First Century Books, 2002.

Day, Nancy. *The Death Penalty for Teens: A Pro/Con Issue.* Springfield, NJ: Enslow Publishers, 2000.

Gaines, Ann G. *Prisons.* Philadelphia: Chelsea House, 1999.

Gottfried, Ted. *The Death Penalty: Justice or Legalized Murder?* Minneapolis: Twenty-First Century Books, 2002.

Hanrahan, Clare, ed. *America's Prisons.* San Diego: Greenhaven, 2006.

Henningfeld, Diane Andrews, ed. *The Death Penalty.* San Diego: Greenhaven, 2006.

Kelly, Zachary A. *Correctional Facilities.* Vero Beach, FL: Rourke, 1999.

The Most Notorious Crimes in American History. Minneapolis: Twenty-First Century Books, 2008.

Oliver, Marilyn Tower. *Alcatraz Prison in American History.* Springfield, NJ: Enslow Publishers, 1998.

———. *Prisons: Today's Debate.* Springfield, NJ: Enslow Publishers, 1997.

Rabiger, Joanna. *Daily Prison Life.* Broomall, PA: Mason Crest, 2005.

Roleff, Tamara L. *Criminal Justice.* San Diego: Greenhaven, 2003.

Russell, Craig. *Alternatives to Prison: Rehabilitation and Other Programs.* Broomall, PA: Mason Crest, 2006

Smith, Roger, and Marsha McIntosh. *Youth in Prison.* Broomall, PA: Mason Crest, 2006.

Worth, Richard. *Probation & Parole.* Philadelphia: Chelsea House, 2002.

WEBSITES

American Correctional Association
http://www.aca.org
The official website of the American Correctional Association represents the oldest and largest international correctional association in the world. This site offers information on the training required to work for the American Correctional Association (ACA) and explains various jobs ACA employees might have.

Archive of Historical Criminological Texts
http://www.crimetheory.com/Archive/index.htm
This is a centralized location for early criminological texts, including writings by Cesare Beccaria and Zebulon Brockway.

Eastern State Penitentiary
http://www.easternstate.org
This is the official website of Eastern State Penitentiary, one of the United States' most historic prisons. This site lists opening hours, coming events, and exhibits at Eastern State, and offers virtual tours and a history of the penitentiary.

Economic Opportunities
http://www.mlfonline.org/developing/ecdev.htm
A faith-based operational ministry of the Memphis Leadership Foundation, Economic Opportunities (EcOp) provides "hard to place" individuals with employment, personal attention, and intensive care. The website offers users contact information and volunteer opportunities.

Federal Bureau of Investigation (FBI)
http://www.fbi.gov
Official website of the FBI offers users breaking news, history and facts about the bureau, tips on how to stay safe at home and at work, and much more.

Federal Bureau of Prisons

http://www.bop.gov

This is the official website of the Federal Bureau of Prisons. The Federal Bureau of Prisons monitors and oversees federal prisons. Users can find inmate and facility locations, learn about job and volunteer positions, and learn about the rights and opportunities of inmates in the federal prisons system.

National Center on Institutions and Alternatives

http://www.ncianet.org

The National Center on Institutions and Alternatives (NCIA) works to break the destructive cycle often associated with correctional systems. The website offers NCIA news, resources, volunteer and job opportunities, and information on the criminal justice system and services of the NCIA.

National Criminal Justice Reference Service

http://www.ncjrs.gov

Administered by the U.S. Department of Justice, the National Criminal Justice Reference Service (NCJRS) is a federally funded resource offering justice and substance abuse information to support research, policy, and program development worldwide. The site includes new and archived official reports on crime and crime prevention, drugs, law enforcement, the justice system, corrections, and more. It includes Q&A sections, publication lists, and external links.

National Institute of Corrections

http://www.nicic.org

The National Institute of Corrections (NIC) is an agency within the U.S. Department of Justice that provides training, technical assistance, information services, and policy/program development assistance to federal, state, and local corrections agencies. The site offers resources for training, an online library, and professional services for corrective agencies.

Stanford Prison Experiment

http://www.prisonexp.org

This website features an extensive slide show and information about this classic study of human behavior in prison. The site provides discussion questions for students.

U.S. Bureau of Justice Statistics, Corrections Statistics

http://www.ojp.usdoj.gov/bjs/correct.htm

The website of the U.S. Bureau of Justice provides statistics on prisons, jails, capital punishment, probation, and parole.

Women's Prison Association

http://www.wpaonline.org

The Women's Prison Association is a service organization committed to helping women with criminal justice histories see new possibilities for themselves and their families. The site offers visitors recent news, information on program services of the WPA, and volunteer opportunities.

PHOTO ACKNOWLEDGMENTS

The images in this book are used with the permission of: © 2005 Roger-Viollet/The Image Works , all backgrounds, p. 2; © Brown Brothers, pp. 9, 26, 31, 33, 47; The Granger Collection, New York, p. 10; © MPI/Hulton Archive/Getty Images, pp. 11, 17; Collection of The New-York Historical Society, neg.#43795, p. 19; AP Photo, pp. 21, 60, 68; © Library of Congress/Hulton Archive/Getty Images, p. 36; © Time & Life Pictures/Getty Images, p. 37; Library of Congress, p. 40 (LC-B2-3310-6); © Popperfoto/Getty Images, p. 43; Humanities and Social Sciences Library/Photography Collection, Miriam and Ira D. Wallach Disision of Art, Prints and Photographs/ The New York Public Library, Astor, Lenox and Tilden Foundations, p. 45; © Archive Holdings, Inc/ The Image Bank/Getty Images, p. 50; © Myron Davis/Time & Life Pictures/ Getty Images, p. 52; © Gordon Gahan/National Geographic/Getty Images, p. 56; AP Photo/stf, p. 59; ©Bettman/CORBIS, p. 63; © Justin Sullivan/Getty Images, p. 73; © Akhtar Hussein/Getty Images, p. 75; © Eastcott-Momatuik/ The Image Works, p. 77; © Brett Snow/drr.net, p. 81; © Paul J. Richards/Getty Images, p. 82; AP Photo/Janet Hostetter, p. 85; © Popperfoto/Getty Images, p. 89.

Front and back cover: © 2005 Roger-Viollet / The Image Works.